A Home Called
New England

A Celebration of Hearth and History

DUO DICKINSON

and

STEVE CULPEPPER

Globe
Pequot

Guilford, Connecticut

Dedicated to Elizabeth Rose Morison Dickinson, now and forever
—Duo Dickinson

Dedicated to my one-of-a-kind: Kathleen Louise Cecilia De Tello Culpepper
—Steve Culpepper

Globe Pequot

An imprint of Rowman & Littlefield

Distributed by NATIONAL BOOK NETWORK

Copyright © 2017 by Duo Dickinson and Steve Culpepper

British Library Cataloguing in Publication Information Available

Library of Congress Cataloging-in-Publication Data Available

ISBN 978-1-4930-1846-8 (hardcover)

ISBN 978-1-4930-1916-8 (e-book)

∞™ The paper used in this publication meets the minimum requirements of American National Standard for Information Sciences—Permanence of Paper for Printed Library Materials, ANSI/NISO Z39.48-1992

Printed in the United States of America

Contents

Introduction

At Home in a New England

Long before the United States was even a twinkle in the Founding
Fathers' eyes, the most ambitious seafaring nations of Europe swooped
in from every angle and divided North America into colonies, each of
those countries determined to remake this world in its own image.

They began landing in the late fifteenth century to claim this New
World for their kings, to institute their religion and their laws, to extract
as much wealth as possible, and, wherever necessary, to subdue by force
the people who were already here. In this way the countries of Europe
gave birth to New Belgium, New England, New France, New Netherland, New Scotland, New Spain, and New Sweden.

While the countries still exist, their American colonies disappeared
along with their empires, leaving only scattered place names to remind
us that they ever were even here. Today the United States is divided
into regions that are less ethnic or political than they are bland compass
points—Southwest, Southeast, Mountain West, Midwest, West Coast,
Mid-Atlantic, Northeast.

Considered early primitive architecture, the Clement Weaver House in East Greenwich, Rhode Island, dates to 1679. It started life like many now-vanished old homes: a one-room structure with a chimney at one end. Additions and updates occurred over the next century with the addition of a lean-to on the rear of the house and an ell added for a kitchen. Upstairs garret rooms offered sleeping quarters for the family who inhabited it.

There's no more New Spain, no New France.

All that's left of the Old World's New World is New England, a clearly defined region of six small states, including the country's very smallest, tiny Rhode Island, which at 1,545 square miles is smaller than Anchorage, Alaska.

Birth of the New England Brand

Despite its modest size, New England's impact has been deeply felt across North America and around the world. In the United States its influence has sometimes been resented (a feeling that New Englanders might interpret as envy), yet that influence remains significant. Although it's not exactly a country in its own right, to many in the rest of the United States, New England bears characteristics of a separate nationality.

New England may be small, but, like its namesake, it's nonetheless a formidable presence.

To best understand and appreciate the character, spirit, and significance of New England is to start far back in the dark, cold past and work forward, along the way roaming New England's countryside and its cities and villages and farms; visiting its houses, churches, factories, graveyards; listening to its people and taking in its distinctiveness. Its difference.

It's a difference that some have called its peculiarity.

At the time of the *Mayflower* landing, while still aboard the ship, the Pilgrims (the male Pilgrims, anyway) drafted and signed the Mayflower Compact, an impressive and tightly written agreement for survival that promised unified effort and work toward a common purpose to survive and flourish in the strange and cold new wilderness.

As you can imagine, their temporary first shelters were little more than lean-tos. The structures that followed were more permanent, though by today's standards hardly habitable. Still the population grew and expanded.

Government was refined to provide rules and laws (and punishments for breaking the laws) to guide behavior and to encourage good morals. This behavior and those rules stayed with them as they expanded throughout the Northeast and began eyeing the vast continent that loomed to their west.

Gradually, settlements were established farther and farther from the original colony. Forests were cleared and streams harnessed. Colonies spread: Providence, New Haven, Hartford, Springfield, New Hampshire, and Maine.

New England prospered and grew, pushing out past the borders of what was properly New England into Pennsylvania and joining the Dutch in New York and eventually the culture and nomenclature of northern Ohio, Indiana, Illinois, and even then farther west. Ultimately, New England was to give the United States place names, governments, and architectural forms that are imitated still, from residences to meetinghouses to town squares modeled on the New England town greens or commons.

On it went, and on it goes.

Along the way New England gave America many things, including town meetings and representative government, the Industrial Revolution, literature, philosophy, great schools. And the terms Puritan and witch hunt.

Many of the images you'll see were found in the extensive archives of the Historic American Buildings Survey, or HABS. The program was created during the Great Depression to serve a dual purpose: It would document with photographs, descriptions, and measured drawings America's houses, churches, factories, bridges, and other structures that were in danger of disappearing. And it would make work during the Great Depression for a small army of architects, draftsmen, and photographers who would accomplish the documenting. Of course it was a national program, but even then it seems to have had a New England tinge—valuing the past and mobilizing the means and energy to preserve and remember that past. And doing it thoroughly and well.

HABS was put aside during World War II and since restarted twice. Today it's going strong with field workers who include architecture and history students. (Since its inception, HABS, Historic American Engineering Record, and, more recently, the Historic American Landscapes Survey, have been administered by the National Park Service, the Library of Congress, and the private sector.)

We concentrate a good bit of the book on the buildings of New England, especially the houses, which anywhere at any time are subtle symbols of a civilization.

Some of the houses documented here were in sad shape when documented eighty-plus years ago and no longer stand. Others soldier on, sometimes looking much worse for the wear; others look pretty much the same; others are lovingly restored.

Many of the houses built since the late nineteenth century have yet to be subjects of HABS recorders, so we show them here in civilian photographs, if you will, photos from homeowners, builders, and architects who created something both designed and built well enough to be proudly left to their children or the great-grandchildren of their children.

This is a sort of family scrapbook of living in New England, a tour of then and now in this cold, frequently standoffish, somewhat distant and memory-prone northeastern neck of the United States. On the

This is a sort of family scrapbook of living in New England, a tour of then and now in this cold, frequently standoffish, somewhat distant and memory-prone northeastern neck of the United States.

pages ahead are the ancient and the new, the tiny and the impressively large, the plain and the fancy. Most especially what you will see is the beauty of ordinary places and structures that are clearly imbued with the DNA of New England.

Along the tour we invariably stray, hearing stories of the people who put down these strong roots—New Englanders who fought the bony soil, built the houses that protected against the unforgiving climate (winter most especially) and continue to carry on, add on and remodel, build anew. From the proud plainness of the oldest to the thoughtful and deliberate design of the newest houses, we roam the six states of New England to see what a home we've made here.

Following are the unique houses, industries, culture, habits, and lifestyle of New England—what it was, what it has shared with the world, what it is now. We glimpse the character and meet the characters found scattered among its modest 62,811 square miles and across its almost four hundred years.

In the Words of a New Englander

In 1839 John Hayward published his *New England Gazetteer, Containing Descriptions of All the States, Counties and Towns in New England*. In his introduction, he writes: "In presenting the public with a Gazetteer of New England, it has seemed proper to make a few introductory remarks of a general nature, on the character of its inhabitants. They may with great propriety be called *a peculiar people*: and perhaps New England and Pennsylvania are the only parts of the new world, which have been colonized by a class of men, who can be regarded in that light."

Hayward proceeds to tick off what made the other colonies different from, if not less than, New England. "The whole of Spanish and Portuguese America was organized, under the direct patronage of the mother countries, into various colonial governments, as nearly resembling those at home as the nature of the case admitted. . . . The same remark, with nearly the same force, may be made of the Virginia colonists: they differed from Englishmen at home in no other way, than a remote and feeble colony must of necessity differ from a powerful metropolitan state."

He found New England to be a different story.

"In the settlers of New England alone we find a peculiar people;—but at the same time a people whose peculiarity was founded on safe practical principles; reconcilable with the duties of life; capable of improvement in the progress of civilization, and of expanding into a powerful state, as well as of animating a poor and persecuted colony."

The weather played a large part in the creation of the New Englander, Hayward found. "Had it not been precisely such an uninviting spot as furnished no temptation to men of prosperous fortunes, the world would have lost that noble development of character which the fathers of New England exhibit. A tropical climate would have made it uninhabitable to Puritans; or rather would have filled it up with adventurers of a different class. A gold mine would have been a curse to the latest generation. Had the fields produced cotton and sugar, they would not have produced the men whom we venerate as the founders of the liberties of New England."

"In the settlers of New England alone we find a peculiar people;—but at the same time a people whose peculiarity was founded on safe practical principles; reconcilable with the duties of life; capable of improvement in the progress of civilization, and of expanding into a powerful state, as well as of animating a poor and persecuted colony."

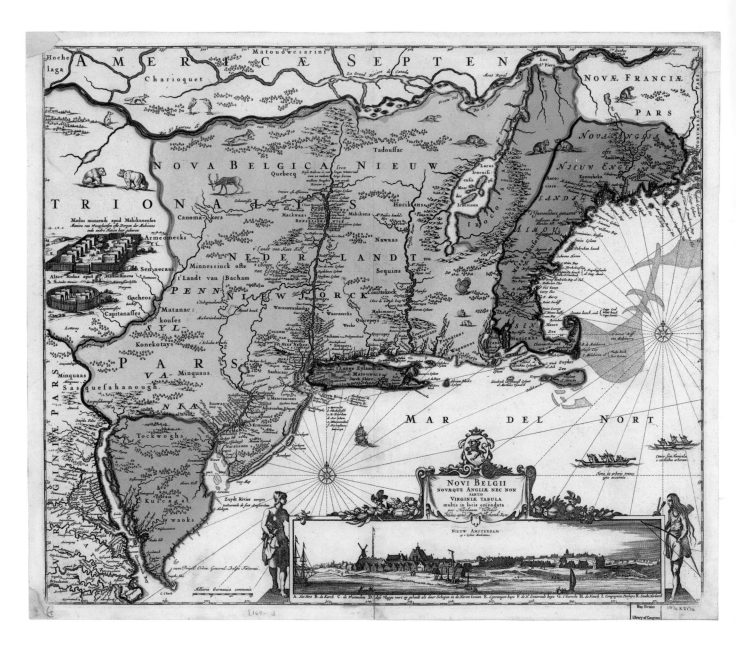

AMERICÆ SEPTEN

Hoche laga

Chario quet

Matouöwesarini

La Grand Riviere de Canada

Mont Royal

Lac St Piere

Quebecq

Tadoussac

NOVÆ FRANCIÆ

PARS

NOVA BELGICA sive NIEUW

NOVA ANGLIA ofte Amidland

NIEUW ENG

Kennebeka

Anco cisco

Lacus Irocoi ensis ofte Meer der Irocoisen

Horikans

N. Pieters handel.

TRIONALIS

Modus muniendi apud Mahikanenses

Alter Modus apud Minnessincos

Canoma kers

Armeomecks

Sennecaas

Gacheos

Capitanasses

Mackwaas

RENSSELAERS WYCK

Mahikans

Nawaas

Sequins

NEDER LANDT nu

PENN

Minnessinck ofte t'Landt van Bacham

Matanac kouses

Konekotays

SYL-

Waranawankongs

Waoransecks

Wecke

Pachami en Wappinges

Sintsinck

Makimanes

Quyrepey

Comittekock

Mericans

NIEUW JORCK

Wiquaeskeck

Quaropey

Pequatoos

Wapanoos

Horicans

Moort Zee

PARS

VA-

Minquaas

Sasquesahanough

NKA

Minquaas

Sanhicans

Matouwancons

Aquanachuque

Tockwoghs

Nuratcons

Sawaen

Emonex

Kus aga

waoks

Zuydt Riviere anders

S. Clerk

Lange Eyland Matouwacs Jorck shire

Staten hoeck

L. Berkens Eyland

Adrian Blocks Eylant

Visschers Eyland

Hinkook

MAR DEL NORT

NOVI BELGII NOVÆQUE ANGLIÆ NEC NON PARTIS VIRGINIÆ TABULA multis in locis emendata per Nicolaum Visscher Nunc apud Petr. Schenk Iun.

NIEUW AMSTERDAM op t Eylant Manhattans

Canoe sive Nargada e certo strata arboren.

Navis in arboris trunco quae excavatu.

Milliaria Germanica communia

A. Het Fort B. de Kerck C. de Wintmolen D. dese Vlagge wert op gehaelt als daer Schepen in de Haven komen E. t gevangen huys F. de H. Generaels huys G. t Gerecht H. de Kaeck I. Compagnies Packhuys K. Stadts Herbergh

Before the Ships Arrived

As long as twenty thousand years ago (some estimates say three times earlier than that) people lived, worked, played, and died in a place we now call New England. It was a place no one in that ancient world could have dreamed would someday be overrun by people from another world, a world named Europe.

What the early natives' world was like before Europeans arrived, observed, and wrote down what they saw, or thought they were seeing, we know remotely from traditions, stories, and objects handed down generation to generation within the many native tribes who staked out their portions of what is now New England. Because these early natives left no written history, we turn to archaeologists, paleontologists, reports of fishermen and explorers, and written accounts from the earliest settlers to fill in what we know about that distant, earlier earth.

Except for place names—and Indian place names are everywhere in New England—little visible evidence exists of the Indian tribes who lived here when the English began landing, settling, expanding, consolidating, and finally and fully taking over.

But look far enough, dig deep enough, and you glimpse those long-ago civilizations. Unlike the Southwest United States, where remains of early native villages and shelters are still quite visible, New England's Native Americans lived in houses built of hide, bark, bulrushes, and branches, all long gone.

Facing page: A 1656 map by the Dutch mapmaker Hugo Allardt shows little visual snippets of life in the mid-seventeenth century, from houses for Europeans to houses for Indians. It's also interesting for the native tribal names given to places that still bear them today. Other names have disappeared over the centuries, along with the Indians who lived there.

New England Places That Bear the Native Mark

Before Europeans anchored in its harbors and invaded its land, all that we now call New England—and its rivers, oceans, animals, hills, marshes, forests, mountains, lakes, coves, caves, meadows, pathways—already had names.

These weren't named for people, not even for the famous and powerful, like many places now are. These names were descriptions of what they were, how they were used, what made them special. They would not have had an Uncasville as they do now, named after the seventeenth-century sachem (the Mohegan chief who allied with the British, who, in turn, helped his tribe became dominant).

Melissa Zobel, an author, historian, and storyteller, serves as both the medicine woman and tribal historian for the Mohegan tribe in a place in Connecticut that today is called Uncasville.

"New England still has a lot of the names, original names. New England has a wonderful remembrance of native words built into its landscape," Zobel explains. "We don't name the earth after people. No people are associated with a place because the place goes on forever. People are transitory. The land and the rivers go on."

The tribes that lived all over today's New England left names everywhere and on all elements of nature around them. "A tribe's name will be synonymous with a place," Zobel said. "When I visit Narragansett, I visit the place. True of all the tribes in New England. When I visit a place, I visit the place and not a person."

So these places were not named for people, like Washington, Allentown, Austin, Cicero, Louisiana, Louisville, Fresno, and so on. "There is no Uncas River, or Occom River—you wouldn't have seen that then." Uncas was the chief, or sachem, who befriended the early Puritan settlers and so made a powerful alliance against enemies.

"The names of the tribes are interesting. Mohegan means 'wolf people.' Other tribe's names mean different things but very often associated with an animal or plant or place," Zobel said. "Some of the names can be very evocative of sounds, sensory qualities of the land—things you could see and hear and feel, rather than a historic personage."

For a full list of Native names across New England, see Appendix A.

Today, what most of us understand about these early people can be boiled down to little more than a chapter in a middle-school history book. Yet during those many thousands of years before concepts of land ownership, written language, firearms, alcohol, and waste arrived in North America, civilization was already well established here.

Not just one civilization, but a lot of them.

Understanding What Was

These first "New Englanders" had families, routines, jobs, and many dialects of the same language, Algonquian. They fished, clammed, harvested fruits and nuts, grew corn and other crops, hunted every type of wild animal, and made maximum use of the land, forests, rivers, lakes, seas—all their many resources for food, shelter, and livelihood.

"They were our first environmentalists," says Dr. Lucianne Lavin, director of Research and Collections at the Institute for American Indian Studies in Washington, Connecticut. "They were sophisticated about nature. They would do controlled burns to make hunting better and clear out the undergrowth, to make the ground better for certain plants to grow. They did management of forests, lands, fisheries."

They also lived in communities of all sizes and in houses of all types, including wigwams, tepees, and longhouses. They had leaders, rivalries, wars, marriages, divorces, friends, and enemies.

Year after year they followed the seasons and the food.

Through [carbon] dating, DNA testing, and careful scientific examination of physical evidence, most of it long buried, what scientists know about early native culture comes from what they've dug up.

A mortar and pestle, or *takhwôkta qinhsunôk*, that has been passed down for nearly three hundred years in the Tantaquidgeon family of the Mohegan tribe. IMAGE COURTESY OF THE TANTAQUIDGEON MUSEUM.

Facing page: A view of the northeast area of North America created by Dutch mapmaker Nicolaes Visscher in about 1690. New Belgium and New Netherland dominate the map while New England gets a thin coastal slice that stretches from Maine to Cape Cod.

Despite the vast amount of objects, relics, and human remains that scientists, farmers, and amateurs archeologists have unearthed, that distant past remains murky and secretive.

Historians know the English, French, and Spanish versions of what's called "post contact" Indian history—what native life and culture looked like to the early European arrivals. Yet the full substance of New England native culture that existed before Europeans "discovered" them remains steadfastly opaque to us, a black hole in history as deep, remote, and as tantalizing as a distant star or the Stone Age itself.

"We only dig up the imperishables," anthropologist and American Indian expert Lavin says. To put it another way, we see only the fragments the early people left behind. What we don't see, she adds, is the "rich texture of their lives."

Lavin has spent a career finding, studying, and understanding the physical evidence of native culture in the Northeast to understand that complex texture.

Importing Europe into the New World

The period of AD 1200–1500 found the New England Indian tribes at their cultural and population peaks. But as Europeans began landing, exploring, claiming, and settling North America, unsurprisingly, native populations began to decline, Lavin said.

Of course the English at Roanoke, Jamestown, and Plymouth were not the first outsiders to visit the New World.

The first Europeans to make contact were the Norse, whose presence mostly was confined to what became the Canadian provinces

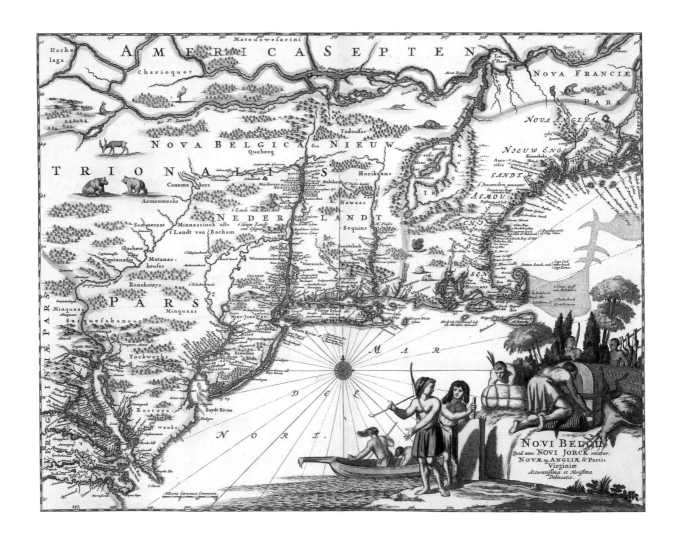

of Nova Scotia and New Brunswick. The Vikings likely traded with
natives they came across—when they weren't slaughtering them.
What's thought to be a Norse coin, though its provenance is unproven,
is a thing called the Maine Penny or the Goddard Coin, which was dug

In My Own Backyard
The Author's Personal Encounter with Native America

In the early 1990s we bought a 1790s Cape in rural Connecticut, a small one and a half story house that needed a new roof, clapboards, gutters, and drains—in that order. The old house had been built into a little hill, so the downspout on one side drained downhill, while the other side drained into the basement. After some research I made a plan to dig a trench that gradually sloped away from the house to daylight out back. Buried perforated drainpipe wrapped in gravel would take the water away from our basement.

After trenching about ten feet from the downspout and to a depth of about two and a half feet, I hit yet another rock. New England is filled with rocks. This one didn't roll over and get scooped up like the others. I got down on my knees and pawed around in the trench and came up with a rounded, oblong, flat rock about three and a quarter inches long by two and a half inches wide, and tapered from a thickness of one inch to about one-quarter inch at its pointy end.

I held it and felt a chill. This was no ordinary dug-up rock. Back in time somebody had worked on this rock, gouging out little dimples on the flat opposite sides of it. Drainage work halted for the day as I sat holding an object—this small piece of granite—that somebody, for some reason, at some indeterminate time in what I figured was a far distant past, had put a lot of effort into.

A woman I worked with was the daughter of a Yale professor who knows about these things, and she showed it to him. The professor's answer came back in a note that said the rock was likely a nut stone and could date back 5,000 to 7,500 years. Nut stones are used to hold a nut in place—let's say a chestnut—so it can get whacked open. Women and children would gather nuts and sit and crack them open for the food inside. For a backyard find, it wasn't bad, he wrote. I've since learned that these are also called cup stones.

This stone, now a bit polished from handling, has sat on every desk I've had over the past twenty-plus years, as it sits now. Here before me is a tool that went missing sometime in the Stone Age and wasn't held again by human hands for as many as 7,500 years. I still feel a chill every time I pick it up.

—Steve Culpepper

Found in Woodbury, Connecticut, this Indian nut stone, which dates as far back as 7,500 years, was used by Indian women and children to hold nuts in place while they were cracked open for their meat, a source of food.

up in 1957 near Maine's Penobscot Bay. If real, it would establish the Viking contact with an area of New England that supported a flourishing native culture, the Penobscot Nation.

After the Vikings came the Spanish, Italians (the very English-sounding John Cabot, sent by Henry VII to explore North America, was born Giovanni Cabato in Venice), French, Dutch, and the English—first in the Roanoke Colony of Virginia in 1586, then Jamestown Colony in 1607, then the Plymouth Colony in 1620, where the English founded what became a series of colonies that eventually melded into a single New England.

In the process of discovery, settlement, and resource exploitation, Europeans nearly wiped out the native population. They did not accomplish this feat by use of their relatively sophisticated weapons, which they did not hesitate to use, but through a means that the greatest killers in history could have appreciated—and found more efficient.

The common diseases that Europeans had built up immunities to over centuries "were new and deadly to the Indians," Lavin said. That could explain why, in 1620, the Pilgrims on Cape Cod found evidence of an empty and apparently abandoned village. Many scholars believe that disease brought much earlier by French or Norse explorers and traders to North America may have spread, sickened, and killed that local population and others.

Alternately, some historians believe that the Indian settlement the Pilgrims found was seasonally abandoned until the natives returned from their inland winter settlement.

Fortunately for the Pilgrims, whatever had become of the Indians in what came to be called Plymouth, those natives who recently had decamped from Cape Cod left caches of seed corn for later planting. Lifesaving seed corn, as it turned out for the English. Although the

Pilgrims came to farm, they were fairly unprepared for the job, because the *Mayflower* was so tiny that each family could bring a very small and limited amount of possessions.

A Plague by Any Other Name

Who had lived in the village? Where had they gone? The National Institutes of Health's journal, *Emerging Infectious Diseases*, explores a theory.

In the few years before the Pilgrims arrived, "most Native Americans living on the southeastern coast of present-day Massachusetts died from a mysterious disease," say the article's authors, Dr. John S. Marr and epidemiologist John T. Cathey. "Classic explanations have included yellow fever, smallpox, and plague. Chicken pox and trichinosis are among more recent proposals."

Marr and Cathey suggest it was none of these classic diseases, nor was it cold, flu, or other common diseases easily transmitted from person to person, for which the Indians had no built-up resistance.

"We suggest an additional candidate," they write: a bacteria-spread kidney and liver disease, "leptospirosis complicated by Weil syndrome," a serious bacterial infection. Marr and Cathey speculate that rats from European ships came ashore and infected "reservoirs and contaminated land and fresh water. . . . Local ecology and . . . practices of the native population favored exposure and were not shared by Europeans. Reduction of the population may have been incremental, episodic, and continuous; local customs continuously exposed this population . . . over months or years."

Standard accounts of the founding of the first New England colony ordinarily fail to mention that disease brought by Europeans

figures des montaignais

David pelle

figure des sauuages almouchicois

Unlike many artists who portrayed the New World in drawings and paintings, Samuel de Champlain had actually been there—multiple times. His illustrations recorded the animals and plants of this strange country, as well as some of the natives. The two couples shown here in Champlain's artwork are the Montaignais, or Innu Indians of Canada, to the left, and the Armouchiquois, an Abenaki tribe from the Saco River area of Maine.

themselves "may have been instrumental to the near annihilation of Native Americans, which facilitated successful colonization of the Massachusetts Bay area."

The English had long ago developed immunities to the disease. The immune systems of the native population were ambushed and helpless against European disease. Natives who had died off by the time the Pilgrims arrived in 1620 could have contracted the disease from rats that had escaped from the ships of "Portuguese, Breton, and Bristol fishermen; Basque whalers; French fur traders; or English codders [fishermen] who had established a presence on the North Atlantic coast since the early sixteenth century," the National Institute of Health (NIH) reports.

The idea of European diseases leading to the death of Indians is not found in most school history texts, which tend to treat the Pilgrims as the first Europeans to set foot on New England soil. Yet well before 1620 Samuel de Champlain noted "100 Spanish sails, 20–30 Basque whalers, 150 French and Breton fishing ships, and 50 English sails along the coast of Newfoundland."

The NIH report adds that "English traders and fishermen had daily contact with indigenous persons but lived on ships or in segregated enclaves on land where salt-dried codfish stations (favored by the English) were built along Massachusetts Bay."

The earliest Europeans found "crippled Indian populations," Dr. Lavin said. "Disease, major epidemics—these could've been plague, smallpox, measles. . . . They were also dying from childhood diseases," she said. "They had no resistance." In other words, measles, mumps, chicken pox, the flu—illness that most of us have experienced and lived to tell about—might well have killed any native without the immunities we take for granted.

Marr and Cathey write that the name "Squanto has entered American history and folklore as one of the last of the Patuxets, the man who assisted the Pilgrims in 1620. He was one of the few survivors of an epidemic that was crucial to the success of the Plymouth and Massachusetts Bay colonies because remaining Indians had little capacity to resist the new settlers."

Two years later, "after having fever and a nosebleed, Squanto died of what was then referred to as 'the Indian disease.'"

Before Sails Appeared on the Horizon

To most historians and native people, the scores of centuries before Europeans arrived in North America are called the "pre-contact" period.

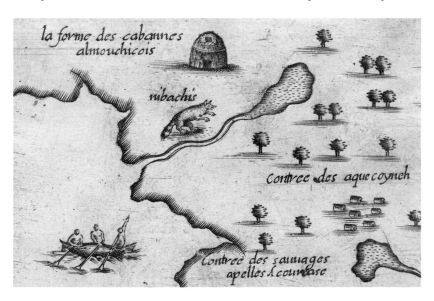

This section from a French map illustrates Thomas Morton's description of native houses. Morton studied and admired the Indians. He wrote that "the Natives of New England are accustomed to build them houses much like the wild Irish; they gather Poles in the woodes and put the great end of them in the ground, placing them in forme of a circle or circumference, and, bendinge the topps of them in forme of an Arch, they bind them together with the Barke of Walnut trees, which is wondrous tough, so that they make the same round on the Topp for the smoke of their fire to ascend and pass through."

Although a Mohegan Indian village would not have had a gravel walk and benches, the rest of this is likely accurate. These Mohegan structures are made of bark built up like shingles and held in place by saplings strapped through holes in the bark. An opening in the center allowed smoke to escape. PHOTO COMPLIMENTS OF THE MOHEGAN TRIBE.

As there were no observant outsiders in North America during those pre-European centuries to chronicle the lives and customs of the people, we go to the earliest written descriptions and to archeologists, scholars, and existing tribes to help create a mind's-eye vision of what New England was like before sails appeared on the horizon.

The European discovery (or invasion, depending on perspective) occurred during the period of North American Indian culture that's now called the Late Woodlands period, a time when the New England tribes had a "very balanced society," Lavin said. "They lived in villages; they were excellent at hunting, fishing, and growing a great variety of foodstuffs."

"There was constantly movement in seasons," said Melissa Tanta-quidgeon Zobel, medicine woman and historian for the Mohegan tribe in Mashantucket, Connecticut (both town and state names are Indian words; *Mashantucket* is the native word for "western," as in the western tribe of Mohegans). "They would generally go back to the same place in summer, a different place in winter. In summer the huts had a different covering than in the winter. In the winter they were covered with heavy bark. In summer they would have a cover of cattails."

An Indian village in New England might have looked a lot like this to early European explorers to North America more than three hundred years ago.

A Happened-Upon Snapshot of Native Culture

Before the English at Plymouth had encountered a single native, they explored the area, dressed in armor and equipped with swords and muskets. On one foray a scouting party discovered fields of recently harvested corn. Going farther they came to the remains of a small village, either an abandoned one or a seasonal one.

As recounted by Edward Winslow and William Bradford, both early governors of Plymouth Colony, the group set about discovering what they could of the mysterious inhabitants—the savages (usually referred to in the English of that day as "salvages") of Cape Cod. What they found suggests both the existence of a well-developed civilization in the modern sense of the word, as well as evidence to the Pilgrims that they were not the first Europeans to set foot on the soil of New England.

In *Mourt's Relation*, a sort of travel book published in London in 1622 and subtitled *A Relation or Journal of the Beginning and Proceedings of the English Plantation Settled at Plimoth in New England*, we read original observations of native life:

> We found a place like a grave, but it was much bigger and longer than any we had yet seen . . . and resolved to dig it up, where we found, first a mat, and under that a fair bow, and there another mat, and under that a board about three quarters long, finely carved and painted, with three tines, or broaches, on the top, like a crown. Also between the mats we found bowls, trays, dishes, and such like trinkets.
>
> At length we came to a fair new mat, and under that two bundles, the one bigger, the other less. We opened the greater and found in it a great quantity of fine and perfect red powder, and in it the bones and skull of a man. The skull had fine yellow hair still on it, and some of the flesh unconsumed; there was bound up with it a knife, a packneedle, and two or three old iron things. It was bound up in a sailor's canvas cassock,

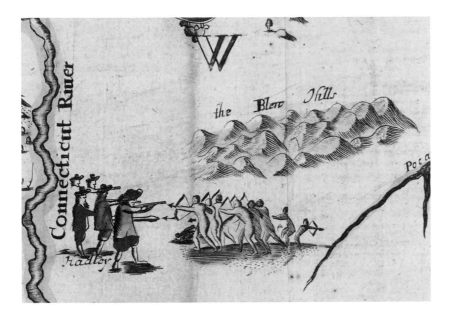

This 1675 map by the prodigious John Sellers, who, like many if not most mapmakers of the day, created by gathering information from sailors and others who had visited and charted the New World, is filled with small drawings and details, such as this standoff between Englishmen brandishing firearms (with their backs to the Connecticut River) and a group of Indians armed with bows and arrows.

and a pair of cloth breeches. The red powder was a kind of embalment, and yielded a strong, but not offensive smell; it was as fine as any flour.

We opened the less bundle likewise, and found of the same powder in it, and the bones and head of a little child. About the legs and other parts of it was bound strings and bracelets of fine white beads; there was also by it a little bow, about three quarters long, and some other odd knacks. We brought sundry of the prettiest things away with us, and covered the corpse up again. After this, we digged in sundry like places, but found no more corn, nor anything else but graves. . . .

Modern Day Mohegan

Melissa Tantaquidgeon Zobel is an author, storyteller, and historian for the Mohegan tribe. She's related on one side of her ancestry, through nearly a dozen generations, to Uncas, a seventeenth-century sachem of the Mohegans. Another strain of her history goes back to the *Mayflower*. Her office in Mashantucket, Connecticut, northeast of New London, is part of the tribal museum and library.

Her aunt Gladys Tantaquidgeon was a Mohegan tribal medicine woman, anthropologist, author, tribal council member, and elder. Beginning in 1934, she worked with the Bureau of Indian Affairs for more than a decade. She published several books about Native American traditional medicine and about healing with plants. In 1994 she was inducted into the Connecticut Women's Hall of Fame. She was the third of seven children born to Mohegan parents, John and Harriet Fielding Tantaquidgeon, on Mohegan Hill in Quinnetucket (Uncasville, in New London County, Connecticut). She was a tenth-generation descendant of the Mohegan chief Uncas.

Melissa Tantaquidgeon Zobel and two of her children.
COURTESY RACHEL SAYET

From Uncas to Uncasville

Uncas was born in about 1588, the son of the Mohegan chief, or sachem, Owaneco. As was commonly done among the powerful in Europe and elsewhere in that day (and likely is still done today), Owaneco arranged a political marriage between Uncas and the daughter of the Pequot sachem, Tatobem.

When his father died, Uncas and the Pequots fell under Tatobem's leadership, which seems to have slowly irritated Uncas into rebelling. When Tatobem was killed by the Dutch in 1633, a Pequot named Sassacus became head of the Pequot tribe and also became de facto leader of the Mohegans. With the help of the Narragansetts, a Rhode Island tribe, Uncas rebelled against Sassacus. However, he and his accomplices failed to unseat the Pequot sachem, which left Uncas as an outcast.

About this time Uncas became friendly with the English. Uncas discovered that Sassacus was planning to attack the English and sent a message to inform Jonathan Brewster, formerly of Plymouth and now of New London, that the Pequots were planning an attack in Connecticut. This began the Pequot War, which the Mohegans won with British help. Later, in King Philip's War, Uncas and the Mohegans came to the aid of the

British against the Narragansetts, who wanted some of the land that the Pequots had won from the Mohegans. The English again came to the Mohegans rescue. Later, in 1675, Uncas and his

Uncas, chief of the Mohegan tribe, executes Miantonomoh of the Narragansett tribe after a 1643 battle in what is now Norwich, Connecticut.

London mapmaker John Sellers—
cartographer to the king—based his
1675 map of New England on a variety
of sources, including lifting images
such as the Indians and their village,
and animals such as beavers, turkeys,
and squirrels, from other maps.

Mohegans came to the aid of the English during their war with the Wampanoag, then later both again attacked the Narragansett.

In the mid-1680s, Uncas died as a sachem, a member of royalty.

"People, especially of the chief's class, intermarried widely with other chief classes in other tribes—the more people you're related to, the better the relations," said Melissa Zobel, historian for the Mohegan tribe.

"Uncas had ancestors from Pequot, Narragansett," she said. "That was done intentionally. You can kind of split New England that way in that sense—a difference between northern and southern New England tribes; they were different but not just because of the climate."

While the various tribes developed their own unique cultures, throughout New England the common native dialects were all forms of Algonquian. In Connecticut, for example, dialects include Hammonasset, Mahican, Montauk, Niantic, Paugussett, Pequot-Mohegan, Podunk, Poquonock, Quinnipiac, Tunxi, and Wangunk.

Indian Reservation and Ferry, Old Town, Maine

The Penobscot Indian reservation and ferry in Old Town, Maine, north of Bangor, in the 1940s.

Beside the Water

Water is vital to all living things, but to the early natives, water was also a source of food, transportation, and culture. Before Europeans arrived, native culture grew up around water—ocean, rivers, and lakes.

"Thinking of waterways is important. New England is a network of both rivers and lakes," Zobel said

For her tribe, the Mohegans, the principal waterway is the Connecticut River. "What is a modern native New Englander? Connections through genealogy and religion. But it's all still along that river—all the people who lived within a distance of utilitarian usage of that river."

At the end of the Connecticut River is Long Island Sound, another source of transportation, trade, and food. "The coast is a connector," she said. "You can easily scoot up both river and coast. When you get to Maine, you've got a miasma of rivers."

Countless rivers, streams, and lakes throughout New England still bear their original Indian names. "Every name in native New England talks about the place," she said. "It tells you something about the environment. Misquamicut means 'the place where the salmon run.' New England still has a lot of the names, original names—New England has a wonderful remembrance of native words built into its landscape."

Native Americans never named places after people. "The place goes on forever," Zobel said. "People are transitory. The land goes on." A tribe's name is synonymous with the place. "This is true of all the tribes in New England. When I visit a place, I visit the place and not a person."

Some of the place names "can be very evocative of sounds, sensory qualities of the land," she said. "These are things you could see and hear and feel, rather than a historic personage."

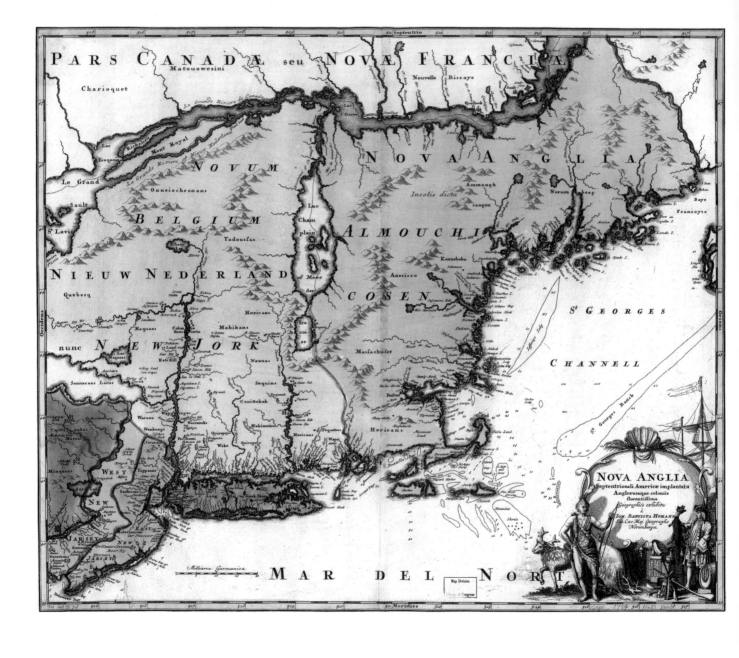

PARS CANADÆ seu NOVÆ FRANCIÆ

Matouowesini

Charioquet

Nouvelle Biscaye

La Grande Riviere de Canada

Le Grand Sault

N O V U M

BELGIUM

NIEUW NEDERLAND

NOVA ANGLIA

Incolis dicta caugen

A L M O U C H I

C O S E N

nunc N E W J O R K

Quebecq

Horicans

Mahikans

Massachuset

Sequins

Conittekok

Makimitios

Horicans

WEST

NEW JARSEY

MAR DEL NORT

Milliaria Germanica

NOVA ANGLIA
Septentrionali Americæ implantata
Anglorumque coloniis
florentissima
Geographice exhibita
à
Ioh. BAPTISTA HOMANN
Sac. Cæs. Maj. Geographo
Norimbergæ.

S.t GEORGES

CHANNELL

S.t Georges Banck

Building a
New England

2

Imagine that a group of Scientologists decide to strap in and rocket off to another planet, where they'll convert the existing native population of that world and build a new, otherworldly paradise around their beliefs.

The reason for the expense and risk? Ideology.

They have jobs, live and work among us, raise their families, and seem extremely ordinary. But within, something is boiling.

Their spiritual beliefs are different from the mainstream, but Scientologists don't live in isolated cults or blow up infidels while proclaiming jihad. Yet, although they're considered harmless, society harbors deep suspicions that Scientology is a fringe value system based on alien concepts. The Scientologists, however, only want a place to practice their beliefs without judgment.

Being a self-sufficient group, well-organized, well-funded, and with a defined hierarchy, the Scientologists feel both alienated and empowered to determine their own destiny. So, using all their resources, they abandon all earthly things, their unbelieving loved ones, everything they've known, and opt for complete autonomy rather than staying on Earth and segregating themselves from those who disapprove or mock.

Now swap "Scientologist" for "Puritan," and change "other planet" to "New World," and you have the essential motivations of the early colonists who escaped the cultural gravity of England and the

Facing page: This Johann Baptist Homann map, published after his death in the early eighteenth century, isn't entirely accurate to scale, topographical features, and geographical relationships, but it is a clear picture of the New World as the first colonists understood it.

Roger Williams
God and Man in Providence

In one century—the sixteenth—at least five (arguably several more) extreme changes in governance happened in England, whipsawing the country between Catholic and Protestant versions of Christianity. God was not just spiritual; God was an agent of government. Catholicism was dominant in most of Europe; the Anglican Church was dissident and homegrown. Whenever either religion was the faith of the king or queen, England's state religion was alternatively looking to the Pope or to the Crown for direction. Politics became very unholy in the name of God. Burning at the stake was common, as were beheadings. Armed conflict and assassinations filled a century with blood in the name of Christ.

Roger Williams, as imagined in this nineteenth-century sculpture, made his own way after tiring of the one-size-fits-all orthodoxy of Winthrop and the Massachusetts Bay Colony. Williams moved to what is now Rhode Island where he created the colony that we now call Providence, named for the act of God that allowed him and his followers to survive. Williams was also generous (as opposed to hostile) to the local Indians.

Roger Williams, born in 1603, was highly educated and well connected, studied religion, and became a chaplain. He confronted corruption in the Anglican Church and expressed his rejection of it in 1629. At the same time another cleric, John Winthrop, was leading a thousand religious dissenters across the Atlantic to form the Massachusetts Bay Colony, a chartered Eden, blessed with rights and freedom of religious expression and self-governance that were guaranteed by the charter, allowing dissention to occur, still under the Crown, but very far away.

Williams left England and a couple of months later joined Winthrop and his flock. Initially Winthrop was happy to bring Williams into the fold. Despite Williams's charisma, or perhaps because of it, Winthrop's welcome turned to rejection. Williams began to object to, then oppose, Winthrop's religious impositions on the Massachusetts Bay Colony. As a significant example, he refused to serve at Boston's First Church because it still was not sufficiently "separated" from the Church of England.

In 1634 the Salem Church chose Williams as its minister—defying the colony's wishes. He and his church were banished from the colony in 1635, suffering extreme, near-death hardship. Williams survived with discrete help from Winthrop, who saw Roger Williams as a smart and jovial fellow Christian who had created a new place to live his faith. Williams believed his survival through a brutal winter was an act of Grace by a loving God.

His survival was virtually providential. Thus he named his community Providence.

Williams also respected and worked with the local Indians at Cocomscussoc (now Kingston, Rhode Island), even creating a dictionary of their language he hoped the returning Christ would use to convert them. After nearly thirty years of trying, Williams finally received a royal charter from King Charles II in 1663. Although the charter was in his name, Williams generously gave up most of the land to his followers and opened the settlement to all. When relations with native populations suffered in the mid-1670s, his settlement was burned, although Williams lived to see it rebuilt.

Back in England, Williams's writing influenced Cromwell, Milton, and Locke. The ripples of Williams's freethinking became manifest in Thomas Jefferson and James Madison's creation of the US Constitution.

Roger Williams was 120 years ahead of the Bill of Rights, but his success saw the entire Puritanical system of religious imposition in New England begin to fade within a few generations, allowing tolerance to become orthodoxy.

Until late in the twentieth century (even to this day), the view of the Pilgrims' arrival in the New World is singularly romanticized: The tiny *Mayflower* is at anchor in the harbor, a boat rowing a crowd of people to a bleak and snow-covered shore. A few Pilgrims are newly landed, while one with outstretched arms waves a benevolent hello to a native who might be Samoset and a fictitious woman who appears to represent an Indian princess. From the cover of "My New England Home" sheet music, words and music by L. Wade.

A sort of early twentieth-century aerial view of Plymouth as it could have looked in its early days in a painting by W. L. Williams.

bonds of the Church of England to pierce the thin coastline that came to be New England.

Over the next ten generations, those sadly unprepared early immigrants built a New World out of a landscape that had existed for as many as twenty thousand years—since the last ice age. It was decisively not England 2.0. What might become fields were filled with trees and, aboveground and hidden below were rocks, rocks everywhere. Winters were brutal during this "Little Ice Age" that stretched from the mid-fourteenth into the mid-nineteenth centuries, according to John Rafferty, associate editor of earth and life sciences at *Encyclopedia Britannica*. One contributing cause might be the "Maunder Minimum," an unusually protracted period of fewer sunspots than is typical, that went from 1645 to 1718. The landscape was filled with multiple native countries that had different languages, borders, and worldviews that these religious zealots did not understand.

A Dangerous Voyage of Faith

An unreasonable faith was how the first colonists survived and ultimately succeeded.

Stepping aboard the aging, boxy, and ill-suited *Mayflower* was no different than stepping onto a Saturn 5 rocket with no training and few tools to head for a foreign planet full of uncertainty along with nearly certain quantities of unknown danger. Reconnaissance missions, like Cabot's, Hudson's, and Champlain's visitations, had brought back reports before the *Mayflower* sailed.

A year after its landing, of the 101 who set sail on the *Mayflower*, the colony's 53 survivors faced an unaccountably cold winter in a land that was not only foreign but hostile. The solid ground of Plymouth, Massachusetts, in the epicenter of the future culture that came to be New England, was as dangerous as the conditions faced by the *Mayflower* bobbing across the Atlantic. The mighty ocean had been crossed occasionally before, but never with the purpose of transplanting people to create a new culture, a theocratic culture, rather than one centered on the supremacy of royalty. Finally, God was the King of Kings. Henry VIII may have created the Church of England, but for the Pilgrims, Jesus and his Father were the only laws they followed.

The Mayflower Compact

The *Mayflower* set sail from London in the summer of 1620 and anchored offshore to wait for the *Speedwell*, a ship bringing English Pilgrims from Holland to accompany the *Mayflower* on the voyage.

After the *Speedwell* kept springing leaks, its passengers jammed into the *Mayflower* and with 101 colonists and about 30 crew, set off for the Virginia Colony. By the time the ship arrived at Cape Cod, it was November, and the weather had become too stormy and unpredictable to safely make the trip farther down the coast to Virginia. So the Pilgrims anchored, waded ashore, and began building shelters for the winter.

However, members of the crew, servants, and tradesmen aboard the *Mayflower* asserted that, because they had not arrived at the official landing place in the Virginia Colony, they "would use their own liberty; for none had power to command them."

The idea of a group of rough sailors having free reign prompted fear in the Pilgrims that such beliefs would lead to disarray. So for the sake of order and survival a social compact was drawn up that all the men signed.

In the name of God, Amen. We, whose names are underwritten, the loyal subjects of our dread Sovereign Lord King James, by the Grace of God, of Great Britain, France, and Ireland, King, defender of the Faith, etc.

Having undertaken, for the Glory of God, and advancements of the Christian faith and honor of our King and Country, a voyage to plant the first colony in the Northern parts of Virginia, do by these presents, solemnly and mutually, in the presence of God, and one another, covenant and combine ourselves together into a civil body politic; for our better ordering, and preservation and furtherance of the ends aforesaid; and by virtue hereof to enact, constitute, and frame, such just and equal laws, ordinances, acts, constitutions, and offices, from time to time, as shall be thought most meet and convenient for the general good of the colony; unto which we promise all due submission and obedience.

In witness whereof we have hereunto subscribed our names at Cape Cod the 11th of November, in the year of the reign of our Sovereign Lord King James, of England, France, and Ireland, the eighteenth, and of Scotland the fifty-fourth, 1620.

William Bradford's transcription of the original Mayflower Compact made a number of years after the actual event.

Where these pilgrims arrived was even more inhospitable than the place they left. The native population, decimated as it was from disease brought by the earlier European explorers, did not want them there but could not repel them. Further adding to their earthly trials, the

What it might have looked like as the men were signing the 1620 Mayflower Compact, in a painting by Jean Leon Gerome Ferris, 1899.

Mayflower's landing was at the edge of a winter made more miserable by the worst the Little Ice Age had to offer.

Like others who followed, the Pilgrims were doing what they knew God was calling them to do, which was to create a place where complete devotion and belief was woven into every act of governance, commerce, and daily life.

Law & Order: New England

From Hartford court records, June 1640:

Ed: Veare of Wethersfyeld is find Xs. For cursing & swereing, and also he is to sitt in the stocks at Wethersfyeld, two howers the next Traying Day.

Willia. Hill of Hartford, for buying a stolen peece of Mr. Plums man, and brekeing open the Coblers Hogshed & Packe, for boath these mysdemenors hes fyned fower pownds to the country.

Nicholas Olmsteed for his lascivious caridge & fowle mysdemenors at sundry tymes with Mary Brunson is adjudged to pay twenty pownd fine to the Country, and to stand upon the Pillery at Hartford the next lecture day dureing the time of the lecture. He is to be sett on, a lytle before the beginning & to stay theron a little after the end.

Edward Veare of Wethersfield is fined ten shillings for cursing and swearing and he is also to sit in the stocks [a device that held the punished locked hands and head in public] at Wethersfield two hours the next Training Day [when members of the militia were required to train or practice drills].

William Hill of Hartford, for buying a stolen article from Mr. Plum's servant and breaking open the cobbler's hog shed and pack, for both is fined four pounds.

Nicholas Olmsteed for lewd attitude and behavior with Mary Brunson is to pay twenty pounds fine and to stand in the pillory [here another name for the stocks] at Hartford the next Sunday, starting just before the sermon and ending just after the sermon.

When Europe Met the Four Indian Kings

These four portraits were painted in London where the "Four Kings of the New World" were taken by the British to see England and to have an audience with Queen Anne in 1710.

Three were Mohawk chiefs of the Iroquois Confederacy, and the fourth a Mohawk, or Mahican, of the Algonquians. The three Mohawk were Sa Ga Yeath Qua Pieth Tow of the Bear Clan, called King of Maguas; Ho Nee Yeath Taw No Row of the Wolf Clan, called King of Canajoharie; and Tee Yee Ho Ga Row, or "Double Life," of the Wolf Clan. The Mahican chief was Etow Oh Koam of the Turtle Clan.

The British set sail from North America with five chiefs, but one died during the voyage. The remaining four met with the queen, were taken throughout London in royal carriages, visited St. James Palace, the Tower of London, and St. Paul's Cathedral.

All of this expense and extravagance on the part of the British was mostly to show the North American Native American chiefs that England was both powerful and willing to help the Indians defend their land against the French and the French Jesuits, who had been converting the Indians to Catholicism. The British were doing their best to rout Catholicism in North America.

These images were painted of "The Four Kings of the New World" for their 1710 trip to England to meet with Queen Anne.

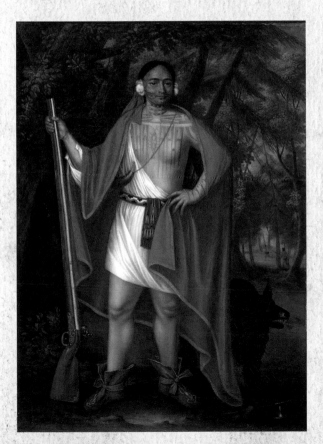

The same irrational faith saw the first Puritans through and beyond the 1620–1621 winter, albeit in reduced numbers. Their fundamentalist faith saw God in virtually every bit of human and natural existence. If death was a part of a greater good, then risking it was reasonable.

The Same Old Rules for New England

Once the first settlers developed the ability to grow food and hunt enough meat to winter over, trade with their indigenous neighbors began to evolve into an economy, and their homes became points of pride and comfort instead of bare, basic shelters.

Regardless of religious orientation, these early New Englanders were still citizens of seventeenth-century England, where houses sported fairly stark medieval peaks, a look that the Pilgrims brought with them.

Steeply pitched roofs arose from medieval reliance on thatched roofing to shed rainwater and snow. The first colonists used thatch, but the far more severe New World climate soon made wood shingles the preferred, if not required, roofing material. The high pitch, now without function for relatively impervious shingled roofs, persisted for nearly a century, when tradition gave way to practicality. Very few of the ancient roof forms survive. But the historical reference was no doubt comforting to the newly minted New Englanders, for whom a proud-to-bursting visual élan was the result.

These side-gabled roofs had little or no eave overhangs and no cornice detailing. Now the survivalist single-hearth chimneys could

So perfectly named, the 400-square foot Peak House in Medfield, Massachusetts embodies the British vernacular style of the homes the colonists created in the seventeenth century. Stark shapes shed snow and water; tiny openings reflect the preciousness of heat and glass; and the indigenous wood and stone remind its inhabitants of "back home."

Like father, like son. The original Peak House was built in 1680 by Benjamin Clark. Thirty years later the house was lost in a fire (or possibly relocated) and the 1711 version was rebuilt on the property by Clark's son, Seth. The historical society that preserves the house says that nine people lived in the house at one time.

Diary of Loss
Jeremiah Bumstead (1678–1747), Boston Glazier

In the early colonies, death was commonplace and always close at hand. Medicines we now buy over the counter would have saved many of the people listed below. Yet life was fragile, disease misunderstood; accidental injuries simply treatable today were often fatal. Meanwhile, on the bright side, God awaited his chosen few.

Here is a snapshot from the early eighteenth century in which a Boston man's diary tersely lists the losses as well as typically brief Yankee descriptions of how he observed his world.

1722

Jan. 10 Extreme cold for 6 days. Mr. Capt. Tuttle, Mrs. Wawxworth, & Mada Fisher, dyed this month.

Feb. 17 Shugger Smith's wife dyde; buryed 21.

Apr. 7 Mrs. Bassett's daughter Woodly dyed at Neviss, about 6 hours before David Bassett arrived there from Curiso.

Apr. 22 Mr. Dramon, ye panell maker dyed between meetings, of ye small pox.

May 1 Mr. Simon Daniell dyed ye beginning of this month.

Jun 11 Mr Bibbins dyed of a soar throat, & running of water from his stomak. Laid in 4 cord of aok wood att 16s on ye wharf, 2s. carting, 10s duty's, 8d carrying in, 3-15-4.

Jul 4 Mr Lamb's son Joshua fell off ye coledg, Stoughton, & dyed ye 15 day.

AUG. Ye Duke of Marlbrough to be buryed on ye 2 of this month, aged 73.

SEP 6 Mr. Barrett's daughter dyed on that day she was to be marryed.

OCT 1 Robert Earlle dyed.

OCT 3 Mr. Dixon's 2nd wife dyed.

*OCT 19 A Mohawk dyed here in town (*New England Courant, *Oct 22, 1722) "Last week one of the chiefs of the Mohawks lately come to town died at the Royal Exchange Tavern in King St., and was magnificently interred on Friday night last. A drawn sword lay on the coffin, and the pall was supported by 6 Captains of the militia. The gentlemen of the council followed next the corps, and then the Justices of the town and the commission officers of the militia. At last followed four Indians, the 2 hindmost . . . who the government had appointed to attend him in his sickness . . . with each a pappoos at her back."*

OCT 28 Mr. Durgin came home. About this time Mr. Griggs & old Mostman dyed. About this time Mr. Walldron went away.

OCT 30 On ye last day of October a schooner burnt at ye end of ye long warff, & a man burnt in her.

be built into massive central chimneys with two, three, or even four fireplaces. More to the west and south of New England, stone-ender gable walls (peaked stone walls on each end of the house) occasionally held fireplaces on outside walls, a showy innovation given the heat loss. Also time and money was spent to lay the brick or stone chimneys into decorative shapes where they sprouted from the roof. The added mass at each end kept homes cooler in the summer and warmer in the winter.

The original and also medieval small windows, often with tiny diamond-shaped panes and inoperable (or fixed), were universally replaced by larger double-hung sashes during the eighteenth and nineteenth centuries, with wood-frame walls covered with board and batten or shingle siding and most often a full two stories rather than a story and a half.

In Massachusetts and Connecticut the second-floor was cantilevered over the first floor wall in what has come to be called a "garrison" detail overhang, often complemented by ornamental trim in acorn shapes. Similar wall overhangs at the attic level are common as well at the gable ends. Full-height cross gables were frequently used on the steeply pitched roofs to add space and light, making deep valleys between opposing roof shapes.

These "post-medieval" houses were originally one room deep and symmetrical, but lean-to rear projections were added to increase first-floor space. By the eighteenth century it became common to shed off the rear of the home with a lesser pitch bay extension, creating the saltbox shape and often doubling the first floor area.

This second wave of colonist building, just after they had literally hit the beach, intentionally mimics modest English domestic buildings that, in the decades immediately preceding the flight of Puritans to

New England's shores, had begun to undergo a transition from medieval to Renaissance structural details.

Soon the need for an old New England house waned for New England's proud survivors. The pride of place began to reflect Yankee ingenuity—not only in thought but in aesthetics, and aesthetics often begin at home sweet home.

Building God's New England

Colonists in the New World began to thrive in the eighteenth century when they overcame the greatest threats to their survival—subsistence, fighting, and disease. Improved commerce removed the need to compete for natural resources.

Everything was going according to God's plan. That plan, however, led the settlers away from the Church of England and its belief system (Anglican services were considered "unserious" as they involved music) and back to a purer form of worship. Baptism was extremely important to all Christians in the seventeenth century. Puritans wanted baptisms only for children whose parents could fully affirm their salvation. Puritans also rejected the common practice of tithing, the automatic contribution of 10 percent of income or wealth imposed by the Church of England. It was not the contribution the Puritans objected to but an obligation imposed by a state religion. For Puritans, giving to the church represented their faithful recognition that all we have we got from God. Therefore, having a little less is no loss.

So when the tiny waves of religious zealots sailed west from England and its Church, they left music and tithing behind. What they brought was extreme faith and a deep commitment to working in the way of the

The Scotland, Connecticut, town green with a traditional gazebo bandstand and cannon. LIBRARY OF CONGRESS, PHOTOGRAPH BY CAROL HIGHSMITH.

Lord. They arrived with few assets beyond faith and the capacity for hard work. They either appropriated land vacated by the native populations diminished by diseases spread by earlier European explorers, or bartered things they had for real estate from the native occupants.

But if all things come from God, then walking the walk of Puritanism meant that their new land was his gift to them, no matter the transactional mechanisms involved. And as long as they were in God's world, what better way to conse-crate a gift from God than by dedicat-ing part of it for God's purposes? As it was, worshipping God was the Puritans' central purpose, so putting him at the center of their lives in this new world was completely natural.

Riches were lacking and, in fact, meaningless to Puritans, but land was central to their survival, and so the most meaningful tithe they could offer God was the best and most central property in their new world. Beginning then, nearly every seventeenth-century New England town had at its very center a place of collective purpose and worship: the town green.

Facing page: The town green in Slatersville, Rhode Island. Town greens provided a public space for gathering and for burying. The Library of Congress description of the photo notes that "the Slatersville Green is in many ways the embodiment of an idyllic New England village with a temple-front church (made of wood and topped by a steeple) overlooking the town green. Around the open space of the green are houses for the overseers of the mill."

John Davenport
Restless in Pursuit of God

Seventeenth-century England was reaping the harvest of a century of religious-born turmoil, where large segments of the Church of England sought greater independence from the Crown, and some churches openly revolted against the state religion.

Born in 1597 to a prominent English family John Davenport was not a firebrand like others. When Davenport's desire to create independent congregational expression within the Church of England failed, he went to Holland in 1633, then sailed to Boston with Connecticut Colony founder Thomas Hooker and other Puritans.

In the New World, Davenport's story becomes as much an "excellent adventure" as a religious mission. His lifelong friend Theophilus Eaton was a successful businessman.

When they reached Massachusetts the two religious seekers and their fellow travelers, mostly merchants not farmers, thought better of an agricultural colony and abruptly sought another place to call home. They packed a sloop in 1638, and ventured west to what became the Connecticut Colony under the Charter of Hooker. Eaton and Davenport landed in an unchartered harbor fed by a river at a marshy area bounded by two small streams nearly at right angles to each other.

The result was New Haven, a place where Eaton built and Davenport preached a theocratic vision that was uncompromised and high-minded. Its high civic intentions were reflected in nine urban mega-squares oriented to the two creeks' intersection. These squares formed New Haven's major roads, and the central square was designed as unsettled open space: a green.

The lives of individuals often manifest the sense of the times they were born into and helped form. John Davenport was the essence of a non-conformist in the Calvinist Puritan tempest that rocked England, and he planted the seeds of New England's unique blend of faith, industry, and innovation.

A portrait of the Reverend John Davenport, who sailed to Boston along with many of his congregation in 1637. A year later he cofounded the Colony of New Haven and was one of the cofounders of the Hopkins School, which still exists. PHOTO COMPLIMENTS YALE UNIVERSITY ART GALLERY.

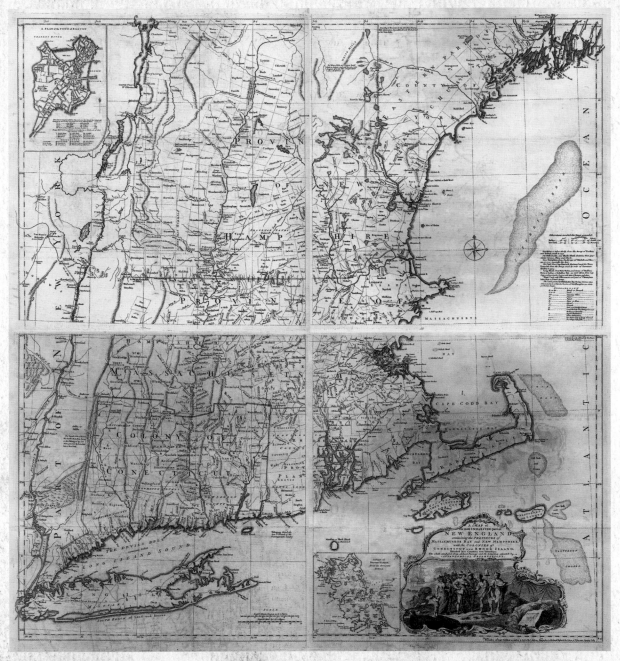

From about 1755, a Thomas Jefferys map "of the most inhabited part of New England; containing the provinces of Massachusets Bay and New Hampshire, with the colonies of Konektikut and Rhode Island."

Greens are not parks. By definition a park is a place of recreation, a place of calm or fun amid the rustle of commerce and culture. For the Puritans, recreation and fun were the work of the Devil. Greens, then, would accommodate the collective agricultural activities of grazing or harvest and become the sacred place of burial and worship. Once survival was assured, a common building could be built on the green for common purposes. This building would be the meetinghouse.

All roads in these new towns emanated from the green or led to it—and thus led to other greens in other villages. Each green was the heart of the first places of New England. If the Puritan life was devoted to only two things—work and worship—the central space and common building each town created and used were simply the manifestation of these two. The green was a place of God's grace in a hostile world and a place that embodied and reflected faith.

As this overwhelming devotion to God waned in subsequent generations, towns grew in number and diversity, and housing, shops, inns, mills, and schools were all built and had land dedicated for their use. Meanwhile, each green remained largely unaffected, the central and abiding cultural and physical focus of New England during its first two hundred years of existence.

On the greens themselves, buildings and landscapes arose that reflected the shift to the earthly activities of a new and energetic culture. Eventually courthouses, libraries, and schools were built that often reposed on what had been empty sacred ground—reserved for graves and cattle grazing.

As the nineteenth century removed the workplace from the home, recreation and sport similarly found their place on the green. Games, strolls, dog walking, concerts, and outdoor markets came to add culture and commerce to what had been the fundamental tithe paid to God in recognition of his mercy.

A Grave Inscription

As late as the early twentieth century, life could be cut short under any number of conditions that now pose little or no threat, and in the example here a death most likely attributable to childbirth. The mid-eighteenth century stone describes a Mrs. Betty Colt who died in October 1765 in New Haven along with "a daughter Aged 6 Hours." Beneath that inscription is her voice from the grave, in rhyme:

Passengers as you pass by

Behold a place where now I lie

As you are now so once was I

As I am now so you will be

Prepare to dic and follow me

Elihu Yale
An Englishman's New England Legacy

The explosion of the Old World into the New was not exclusively the result of those seeking religious expression. The New World, for later immigrants to New England, was not a religious refuge. Instead, the eighteenth-century New World was an explosion of economic opportunity, and thus governments leapt into conflicts for territory and especially the trading routes and business opportunities those territories leveraged.

Although Elihu Yale was born in 1649 in Boston, when he was three his parents took him to England, where he was educated in London. In 1671 Yale found himself employed by the extremely profitable East India Company as one of its governors of Madras. Although he helped found a hospital there, the real result of Yale's talents was extreme, even perhaps extra-legal financial success.

His greedy over-the-top side-dealing (or more likely double-dealing) got him fired from the East India Company, but not until his amassed personal fortune eclipsed the negative impact of his termination. In 1699 he returned to London.

It turned out that his generosity matched his avarice, and soon his reputation for giving spread to New England. In 1718, Cotton Mather, a Harvard man, contacted Yale seeking money to construct a building in the New Haven Colony for the new Collegiate School that was moving from Saybrook, Connecticut. (Yale had previously sent thirty-two books to the school in 1713—a generous gift in those times.) Yale arranged for a large container of goods to be sent to Connecticut, where it was liquidated for almost £600, which funded construction of New Haven's new school building.

That seminal support made the students and faculty feel that their Old World benefactor should be given recognition, so almost twenty-five years after Yale's death, the small but growing school in the former theocratic utopia of New Haven Colony renamed itself Yale.

Yale and rival Harvard's namesake, John Harvard, could not have been more different. Harvard was a Massachusetts Bay Colony cleric who died devoted to the New World and bequeathed his estate to found a college in the new Cambridge. Self-enriching Londoner Yale tossed some books and a box of loot across the Atlantic, and the twain's grateful recipients have maintained their exceptionally effective branding for all the centuries since.

Born in Boston in 1649, Elihu Yale died in London in 1721. In the early eighteenth century, Yale donated 417 books and other goods to efforts in New Haven to construct a new building for a fledgling college, which was named for him. Eventually the school, the Collegiate School of Connecticut, became Yale College. PHOTOGRAPH COURTESY OF YALE UNIVERSITY.

Soon trees, walks, benches, memorials, flagpoles, and fountains were put down to subtly convert greens into places that venerated a distancing past. While these gifts of cleared land to the Almighty had been created to serve his purposes, New England greens transitioned to become preserved and venerated oasis places and portals into the time of their creators, rather than to the Creator.

Like the first seeds the colonists planted, the love they had for God grew in their successors to become a love of freedom. From that grew a country that made freedom to worship, or not, the law of the land. This center of each town's physical growth, its green, became a place that today quietly references those centuries of faith in God and freedom.

In the seventeenth century, the idea of a state religion was fundamental to coordinating every aspect of New England life. The Bible and God's word were the defining baseline of every aspect of the first generations of New England's creation.

As God's plan was becoming manifest, and as cattle, farms, and currency replaced hunting, gathering, and bartering, secondary aspects of life would compete with the essential puritanical life. Religion could build glories such as beautiful places of worship, versus the original fundamental simplicity of "when three or more are gathered together." Governance could have two functions, God and law, and become civic.

Continuing God's Work

Puritans concluded that God was commanding them to defeat their "heathen" enemies by any means necessary. For the English, all restraint in war, all notions of "just conduct," applied only to secular warfare. In a holy war, anything goes. Ministers urged their congregations to "take, kill, burn, sink, destroy all sin and Corruption, &C which are professed enemies to Christ Jesus, and not to pity or spare any of them."

Such a policy, then as now, breeds nothing if not merciless retaliation. As a Boston merchant reported to London, the Indians, in town after town, tortured and mutilated their victims, "either cutting off the Head, ripping open the Belly, or skulping the Head of Skin and Hair, and hanging them up as Trophies; wearing Men's Fingers as Bracelets about their Necks, and Stripes of their Skins which they dresse for Belts."

At center stage in native chief King Philip's (or Metacomet's) War was a militia captain named Benjamin Church. Born in Plymouth in 1639, Church fought in many of the war's bloodiest engagements. Among them was the "Great Swamp Fight," in December 1675, in which English forces killed thousands of Narragansett women, children, and old men hiding in a makeshift fort constructed in the middle of a Rhode Island swamp for their protection. Most died after the English set the fort on fire. (One Boston poet wrote, "Here might be heard an hideous Indian cry, / Of wounded ones who in the wigwams fry.")

In August 1676, after Philip was shot, Church ordered his body drawn, quartered, and decapitated, whereupon the colony declared a special day to give thanks to God for their signal victory. Philip's head was placed on top of a stake in the middle of town, where it remained for decades and where it rotted down to the skull.

The Rocks of Ages
Henry Whitfield's Puritan-Era Home

Born in 1597 Surrey, now part of greater London, the Reverend Henry Whitfield felt the calling and in 1639 gave up his post as rector of St. Margaret's Church in Ockley, southwest of London, and set off for New England with two dozen other Pilgrim families on the ship *St. John*.

Just after landing on September 29, 1639, these first residents—mostly farmers—set themselves down in Guilford, Connecticut.

In his 1877 history of Guilford, Ralph D. Smith writes that "Henry Whitfield, Robt. Kitchel, William Leete, William Chittenden, John Bishop, and John Caffinge, in behalf of themselves and others, who . . . had come out to New Haven the same year . . . were now resolved to make a settlement at this place. At the time of the purchase it was understood and agreed that the deed should remain in the hands of the planters, until a church should be formed in the town, to whom it should be given and under whose superintendence the lands should be divided out to those who were interested in them."

The group of Pilgrims bought the land from the local Indians in exchange for "twelve coats, twelve fathoms of wampum, twelve glasses, twelve pair of shoes, twelve hatchets, twelve pairs of stockings, twelve hoes, four kettles, twelve knives, twelve hats, twelve porringers, twelve spoons, two English coats. The Indians agreed to remove, and it was generally understood that they did remove to Branford and East Haven. An article, however, in the Guilford records suggests that a number of them were permitted to remain for a time. . . . The English settlement commenced immediately after this purchase on the grounds now included in Guilford borough, the plain and some lands near the sound having been cleared by the natives and prepared for cultivation."

Whitfield was the group's minister. Construction on Whitfield's house began immediately but had to be put on hold for the winter. When completed, it contained a great hall and north fireplace made by locally quarried stone, which make the walls nearly two feet thick. Joists and rafters were hewn from local oak, and the floors and interior walls were built with pine.

In late 1657 Whitfield returned to England, where he is buried in Winchester Cathedral, where he now shares consecrated earth with Izaak Walton, Jane Austen, Cnut the Great, and William II.

The Henry Whitfield House in Guilford, Connecticut, dates to 1636 and is the oldest house in the state.

The Henry Whitfield house was remodeled in 1868 to be opened to the public as the state's first museum. It has been restored in 1902–1904, in the 1930s, and again within the last decade. It was declared a National Historic Landmark in 1997 and a State Archeological Preserve in 2006.

Today the Connecticut Commission on Culture & Tourism maintains the Henry Whitfield State Museum, which is a National Historic Landmark and a State Archaeological Preserve. It's also the state's oldest house and New England's oldest stone house.

William Goffe rallying the men of Hadley, Massachusetts, in defense of an Indian attack during King Philip's War.

Learning How to Live in This New World

The extreme risk of immersing themselves in the unknown wilderness of New England meant the first act of seventeenth-century settlers was survival. They built fragile tiny homes out of immediately available materials—fieldstone, green wood, earth. For a generation or two they hung on by their fingernails, making better homes, cultivating fields, building herds, finding dependable supplies of drinking water, rearing children that lived past infancy.

A view of Boston toward the southeast showing ships in the harbor about 1730 by British cartographer John Carwitham.

Once physical survival was established, the spiritual raison d'être of putting themselves at mortal risk in this New World could receive some communal attention. Presumably worship happened frequently, in whatever structures were available, at least until there was relative stability of sources of food, shelter, and clothing and thus time to build a dedicated house of worship. Relative stability, or security, meant that each of the town-states that had come to this wild world could manifest their common desire for full religious expression. In the eighteenth century these autonomous communities could raise money and dedicate physical labor for more than sustenance.

The government, the people, would pull together and actually build the architectural center of each town: the meetinghouse.

It wasn't just the town hall. It wasn't just the church. The meetinghouse was the tallest, best-situated structure in each village, set on the town greens that formed the civic heart of commerce, social life, civic debate, and the grazing of cattle and marshaling of militias. After basic survival was assured, the building of meetinghouses accelerated all through New England.

Meetinghouses fused social, cultural, governmental and spiritual life into one architectural synthesis.

Meetinghouses fused social, cultural, governmental, and spiritual life into one architectural synthesis. They were whitewashed to a sparkling newness when most buildings were weathered wood. Walls were often two stories tall, built at one big barn raising, versus homes built piece by wing.

Building Proof of Their Faith

New England's first English inhabitants based almost all their actions on their religious beliefs. Fleeing from the most radically reformationist country in the Old World (the one where the king of England replaced

the pope), these reactionaries took the Protestant ethic to new extremes. They risked life and limb to have a direct relationship with God.

Pilgrims, Puritans, Quakers, the early Baptists took what they owned and left behind everything they had known, rejecting a century of religious revolution to walk the walk (or sail the travail) to the New World, a place of unfathomed danger.

Where late sixteenth- and early seventeenth-century settlers immigrated to Virginia for economic reasons, these religious radicals landed in New England for spiritual reasons, to speak to God directly, bypassing the intermediaries of pope and priest.

A distinctive example of New England settlers' motivations was the New Haven Colony in Connecticut. The New Haven Colony was created on April 24, 1638, when a company of five hundred English Puritans led by the Reverend John Davenport and Theophilus Eaton, a wealthy London merchant, sailed into a large harbor (see page 44). The location was propitious for building a "city of God." The first community was made of nine large square blocks centered on a central square. This green became an all-purpose open urban space.

In New Haven, the central green did not get a religious structure until long after Eaton and Davenport were gone. Three churches were built in the 19th century, including, amazingly, one for the Church of England, which had come initially in 1757, after the town's Puritan founders' power had faded.

The interiors were as fine as the finest home, but the Puritan ethic of rejecting ornament, music, and expression meant their clean lines and simple details captured daylight with a stark purity that was a perfect symbol of complete faith in the Light of God.

The Rockingham Meetinghouse in Rockingham, Vermont (top left and right) was built between 1787 and 1801 to serve the religious and civic needs of the community. The Royalton Meetinghouse—also called the town house—(bottom left) was constructed in 1840 on the town green in Royalton, Vermont. The interior of the Elder Ballou Meetinghouse in Cumberland Hill (bottom right), Rhode Island, looking toward the pulpit and Elder's bench.

LIBRARY OF CONGRESS

The Oldest Church in New England
The Old Ship Church

Everybody knows it as the Old Ship Church, but its official name is First Parish in Hingham, Unitarian Universalist. By any name, it's the oldest church in New England, where old matters and where the oldest carry an extra weight of history.

And according to the *New York Times*, it is "the oldest continuously worshiped-in church in North America."

Founded in 1681 and built in the English Gothic style, it came along in stages. First a timber frame was built (the curved roof timbers were hand-cut with an ax). Then, in 1730 and 1775, side galleries were added.

Like most New England meetinghouses, the Old Ship Church served both as a church and as a place for the town together to discuss civic matters. "The simple meeting house design is itself emblematic of the principles on which our country was founded. Hingham is home to this matchless piece of American history, recognized as a National Historic Landmark. The Old Ship Meeting House is a monument to the past, and an inspiration for the future," according to the church's website.

The southeast elevation of the church.

A detail of a pew end.

The central aisle looking toward the pulpit.

The balcony railing on the Old Ship Church.

Pulpit windows on the church's northwest side.

An axial view of the church pulpit with sounding board above, which helps project the voice of the speaker.

The abstraction of the sacred became a foil for the profane as the Sunday Sabbath gathering was often reciprocated by the regular town meeting, where all the jealousies, legalities, and bean counting rendered these civic structures into sounding boards for the collision of culture, commerce, and Christianity. The lofty virtues of sacrificial love in the hope of grace had its flipside in the self-interest, petty politics, and personal vendettas every municipality legislates to regulate.

Since World War II, in Europe and New England, religious belief has significantly waned as a cultural focus. Perhaps centuries of familiarity has led to contempt. Many meetinghouses have become museums, as government outgrew its tight confines and religious life shrank away from the public square. Many families who once held religious observance central to their lives no longer set aside the Sabbath to worship. Instead of attending to a "day of rest" in any brand of religious venue, time is spent in Starbucks, shopping malls, or sports arenas.

White clapboard churches on town greens used to symbolize New England Christianity. Now they lend the region historic gravitas, while their role in religious life declines. Meetinghouses remain deeply compelling but more as touchstones to a time of courage and trial amid extreme adversity, when people risked everything to be with their God, and away from their king.

We see the extreme effort to build the biggest, nicest building in town to express a devotion to freedom found in common interest and belief, the uniquely American vision of bottom up determination in faith that everyone—everyone—was entitled to "life, liberty, and the pursuit of happiness." The Revolutionary War turned that belief into a government on a national scale. Creating a federal system based on a social dynamic that was test-driven in every meetinghouse in New

England is a natural extension of how America came to be, long before the Founding Fathers were born.

New England Redefined

Although the English eventually got the actual land, the Dutch were the great European mapmakers of the seventeenth century. These colorful and detailed maps were not simply works of art or even navigation; the Dutch used maps to redefine and reorder reality.

In areas where the English were clearly in control, the mapmaker "deeds" the land to his country. He grants England most of the land east of the Connecticut River but assigns ownership of much of the rest to "Neder Landt" and the northernmost parts to New Belgium, and gives the French a bit of what's now Canada with the label "Nova Franciae." Overall, it establishes the contest being waged between the great European powers of the day.

Names of Indian tribes are also labeled throughout, and images of the natives and portraits of some of the wildlife a Dutchman might find roaming the hinterlands of this strange but clearly valuable New World are included.

Not all of New England began as English. The Dutch, French, and Portuguese each variably staked claims to large portions of the northeast. However, to the settlers go the spoils, and the English made it a point to create more strategically placed settlements than any other European competitor.

The map titled "Belgii Novi, Angliae Novae et Partis Virginiae" (New Netherland, New England, and parts of Virginia) was published

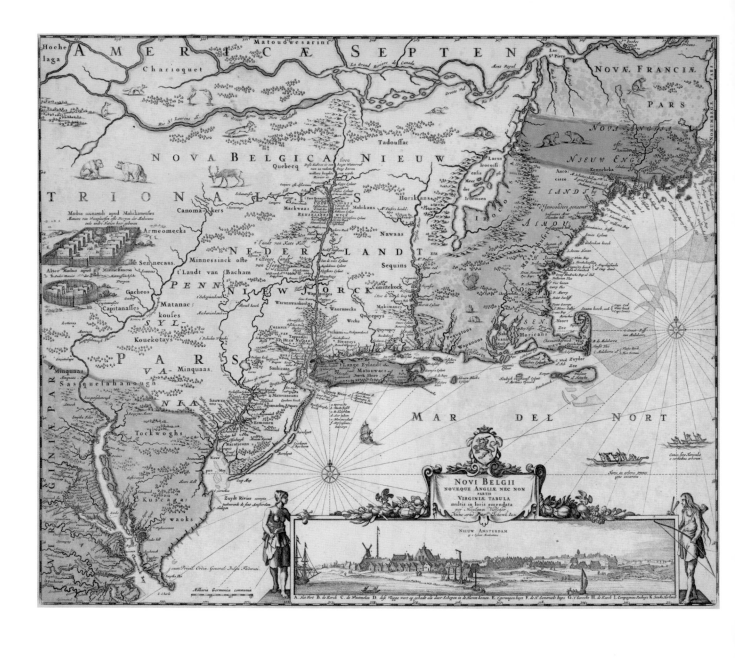

in 1650 from earlier maps and multiple sources from the English, French, and Dutch. Although it was propaganda for Holland and its New Netherland colony, it still shows fairly clearly the early English colonies of the Atlantic coast.

Like the British, Spanish, and French, the Dutch explored on behalf of companies chartered by the country's rulers both to find new markets for their goods and to set about harvesting the untapped riches of the New World. For the Dutch, the chartered company was the Dutch West India Company.

Not sold to Great Britain until later in the century, New York is labeled as "N. Amsterdam." It also shows "Nieuw Nederland" (the Dutch colony) stretching across most of what's currently New England, including all of Connecticut, Vermont, and Rhode Island as well as most of Massachusetts and New Hampshire—that is, everything between the Delaware River (Sassquessahanoughs) and a slice of the East Coast given over to the English.

Steering a Course toward Commerce and Independence

Beyond each of the town-states that popped up along the coast, spread into the interior, and manifested the promise of religious freedom, the success of New England's seventeenth-century starting point was radically redirected in the eighteenth century as civilization and commerce became more important than its founding ideology.

New England's early Puritan pioneers faded as crops grew, homes were built, towns created and expanded, and families flourished in a

On a Mission for God
Samson Occom

His name is spelled most commonly Samson Occom. He sometimes appears as Samson Occam, Samson Occum, and, appropriately for an Indian Presbyterian born in colonial Connecticut, his name was sometimes spelled Samson Ockham. The Connecticut-born Mohegan also appears in some texts as Samuel Occom.

He was born in 1723 New London, Connecticut, educated at Eleazar Wheelock's "Lattin" School (where he learned both to read and speak Hebrew), and set himself a goal of converting his fellow Native Americans to Christianity. After becoming a preacher, he spent a couple of years trying to Christianize the Six Nations of the Iroquois in upstate New York, which didn't take. So he returned to Professor Wheelock in Lebanon, Connecticut, who had started an Indian charity school.

Having become an influential Mohegan Presbyterian preacher, Occom was sent by Wheelock to London with a goal of raising money for the school.

Between February 1766 and July 1767, Occom delivered several hundred sermons and became a celebrity curiosity who pulled in large crowds eager to see a Native American and to hear his preaching. During his time in London, Occom drew large crowds wherever he preached, meanwhile raising more than £12,000 (which converts into about $2.7 million, today) for Wheelock's school. Everybody from George III on down donated. Meanwhile, as part of his arrangement with Wheelock, Occom's family was to be supported and cared for while Occom was in England.

On his return, Occom discovered that his family had not been taken care of and that Wheelock had taken the money and founded Dartmouth College to educate the Englishmen, not the Indians as promised.

Occom and his family moved to live with the Mohegans, where he helped organize Christian Indians into a new tribe in Connecticut. However, land once so plentiful was growing scarce, and the tribe moved to Oneida, New York, where they built a new town they called Brothertown. With more emigration by the Native Americans in Connecticut and Massachusetts, the tribe created the nearby town of New Stockbridge, where on July 14, 1792, Occom died. He was buried in nearby Deansboro, New York.

Reverend Samson Occom, the Connecticut Indian Presbyterian, dating from between 1828 and 1840.

place of relative freedom. The religious zealotry of New England's first immigrants was a victim of its own success. Abstinence had a short shelf life, theocracy gave way to freedom of religion, and entrepreneurship flourished in a place where class became less important than innovation and hard work.

When enough people could produce more than they consume, things get sold, markets made money and attracted more people who wanted to make money. Profit replaced salvation.

New England's port cities grew fast. Beyond mere ports for arrival and distribution, the ports connected the coastal settlements with roadways where the as-yet-unalterable waterways fell short. By 1673, the Boston Post Road connected the two best ports in the New World, New York and Boston, further allowing European settlement in the untainted wilderness of New England, where roads made clusters of isolated villages into states and then into something more resembling a country, economically as well as culturally.

At the named eastern terminus of the Post Road, Boston is the best natural port in New England. It incorporated as a town in 1630 and as a city in 1822. Like every other town, Boston began as a homesteading community, but as the rest of the world began buying what New England made, and people wanted a piece of the profit in the making, Boston quickly grew to become a hotbed of economic and political muscle.

Unlike Mother England, in New England ability meant more than the class you were born into. Also unlike the homeland, getting rich within one generation was a real possibility. While it was less risky on every level to come to New England in the eighteenth century than the seventeenth, abandoning all the luxuries of home breeds a devotion to success that most don't experience when all around them is safety and comfort.

Built about 1819 in North Andover, Massachusetts, the tiny house is one story with a single hip roof. Except for the financially well off, many houses were uncomfortably small by today's standards and often housed large families.

This rectangular classic Cape Cod structure in Truro, Massachusetts, was made as a utility building to hold wood. It has a small loft as well as an attached shed addition and dates from the early nineteenth century.

Built after 1637 by Captain William Pierce and sold in 1647 to Deane Winthrop, son of John Winthrop, founder and former governor of the Massachusetts Bay Colony.

The House of Seven Gables, the prototype for Nathaniel Hawthorne's 1851 Gothic novel of guilt and mystery, including witchcraft and other elements of the paranormal. The house belonged to his cousin Susanna Ingersoll.

You naturally want to protect the risk you've invested in or taken. England began to make money off the backs of those who abandoned its tightly ruled shores by exacting tariffs, taxes, and restrictions on the wayward subjects. Naturally, the British navy and army did their parts to protect these now profitable new colonies both from other European powers and also from certain threatening Indian tribes.

The Jane Dillon House in Easton, Connecticut, photographed in the 1930s, was built about 1710 as a three-room, end chimney saltbox-style house with a loft.

Hearth and Home

3

How We Lived Then

In colonial times, before the Industrial Revolution, most men were farmers. Farmers always need farmhands, so having lots of children was a common practice for producing the field hands of the future. In addition to the parents, as many as eight or ten children might have lived in the small house and, if an older son got married, his wife and, eventually, baby might live there, too.

Include in the list a servant girl, who usually lived with the family, and soon this hypothetical group adds up to as many as fourteen or fifteen people in one tiny house. These would be 400–600 square feet in the single-cell house in which the fireplace and chimney might take up a third or fourth of that space. Often a second-floor loft would provide sleeping quarters for children and servants. (For context, today it's not unusual for a master suite comprising bedroom, bath, and walk-in closets to be five hundred or more square feet.)

Add a hungry and unwelcomed British solder to the mix, and living conditions would have been that much more unpleasant.

Built in 1637–1641, the Jonathan Fairbanks house in Dedham, Massachusetts, is believed to be the oldest timber frame house in North America. It is owned, maintained, and operated by Fairbanks Family in America, Inc., a genealogical membership organization.

Built in the late seventeenth or early eighteenth century, the Benjamin Abbot House was the home of Benjamin Abbott. During the witchcraft panic of the 1680s, Abbott accused his neighbor Martha Carrier of witchcraft; she was hanged in 1692. One rumor is that Abbot made the accusation so he could gain control of Carrier's property.

An Architect for a New Era

A variant of Georgian architecture, the Adam style is a simplified version of neoclassical architecture named for architect Robert Adam, the eighteenth-century son of prominent Scottish architect William Adam. The style's clean lines became very popular in New World America, which is ironic because Adam was appointed Architect of the King's Works for American tormentor, George III, only to leave that post in 1768 to devote more time to his elected office as member of Parliament.

The earlier style of Georgian architecture was based on Renaissance motifs that architect Adam called "ponderous" and "disgustful." Adam preferred starker, simpler lines, less decoration, and simpler shapes. His rejection of Georgian architecture's elaboration of ancient classical details and motifs could be due to the obligatory aristocrat's European tour, which followed his formal education.

This house was owned by Connecticut's Patriot governor, Jonathan Trumbull. Trumbull was born in Connecticut, educated at Harvard, worked as a storekeeper, speaker of the Connecticut State House, and a colonel in the state militia. During the Revolution, Trumbull was an advisor to Washington and served as paymaster of the Continental Army. Washington called Trumbull "the first of the patriots."

Seeing the original Greek and Roman antiquities up close and in detail, Adam came to feel that Georgian architecture misappropriated the purity and clarity of the ancient architecture.

For most of us, the distinctions Robert Adam advocated were subtle but appealed to America's puritanical taste in simpler lines over the more elaborate Georgian style. The results were evident in the small simplification of elements such as the shape of a front door's transom window, the clarity of dental trim in eaves and trim surrounds, and the rigorous consistency of window organization, all ganged in sets of three.

With simple house shapes, wholesale and local symmetries are the rule. But symmetry uses mostly five openings (versus three or seven) on the all-important centered front face of a house—a door in the middle and a pair of windows on each side, all equal distance left and right. Make no mistake, however: The means and methods of Adam-style building require significant resources to execute.

Like Georgian architecture, the Adam style had been the cutting edge of England when it first flowered here. It was the preferred nineteenth-century way to detail and arrange the simple parts of post-colonial homes of the wealthy. There were no poor-man's or working Adam-style farmhouses but vast and wealth-making Southern plantations. Yes, gentlemen's farms, for sure, and, of course, the country home could be Adam style, but the growing American middle class aspired to be rich enough to afford things like Adam-style architecture, too.

In that way, the reach to be "as good as" British architecture drove architects in New England to first imitate and then create a style of building that was, it turns out, all theirs. Adam style was one of the launching pads for that accomplishment, weaning the Englishness from New England aesthetics.

It was during this era that the first true architects appeared on the American scene. Charles Bulfinch of Boston and Samuel McIntire of Salem, Massachusetts, led the way in New England. Architecture was of course just one of the many vehicles that America used to find itself in the nineteenth century. It was also one of the brightest mirrors of the new native culture.

The Colonial Mansion
of the King's Mast Man

Pinus strobus, the great white pine of the upper Midwest and Northeast and the largest conifer in New England, grows in Maine and New Hampshire to 150 feet or more with diameters of up to a maximum of 40 inches.

In colonial days it grew even larger.

It was that pine—those trees—that brought former Royal Navy Captain George Tate, fresh from a promotion to Senior Mast Agent

The exterior shows the symmetrical, even formal style of the Tate House's Georgian architecture.

Its massive brick chimney tops the gambrel roof of the structure, which includes a small addition.

The beautifully crafted china cupboard with its fan-shaped carving is a centerpiece in the home's dining room.

Raised paneling, fluted pilasters, and elegant crown molding grace the dining room.

A head-on photograph that displays the essential symmetry of the Georgian design.

A staircase was turned into a work of art with exquisitely turned spindles and beautifully curved banisters turning across the raised-panel wall and up to the second floor.

The kitchen in such a grand house was a workroom for cooking with the use of the large, walk-in- size fireplace—and servants.

for the British Royal Navy, to Maine in the 1750s. The huge, straight, strong trees were among the best material for masts anywhere on the planet. The Royal Navy needed a constant supply, and it was Tate's job to keep the trees coming.

While in Maine, Tate built the grandest house in the Portland area, high on a knoll overlooking the Fore River, the waterway on which the fallen white pines traveled to the sea and to the ships that took them to the ship-building ports of England.

While at work on the king's business, Tate built for his family a home that offered proof to the locals of his position. The Tate House still stands as a historical museum operated by the National Society of Colonial Dames. The house, with its odd gambrel roof containing clerestory windows, was built in 1755 for George and his wife, Mary Tate. It was meant to be, and still is, obviously the home of a man of means.

As it would have been in 1755, the Georgian Tate House is still made of unpainted clapboards, though the trim is a now a historic dark yellow. It also has those clerestory or dormer windows set into a vertical wall in the sloping gambrel roof—which was then, as it is now, a maintenance headache because of water and snow that accumulates on a roof of that shape.

During his time in New England, Tate and his men would scour the backwoods of Maine and neighboring New Hampshire for the huge pines. When they discovered a white pine of the needed dimension, they marked it with the "king's broad arrow," an arrow-shaped hatchet-slash branding that warned colonials against harvesting these "mast" pines.

Naturally, New Englanders were resentful and cut the trees anyway, a jailable offense. The first flag of New England features a red background with a white pine rising prominently in the upper left corner.

At Home in New England

Today the average size of a house is 2,598 square feet; in the eighteenth century, this would have been in the top tier of homes, those of the wealthiest and most prosperous citizens of New England.

The majority of homes then were very much smaller, often with only one or two rooms and an attic, or loft, usually a place for the children and a servant to sleep.

In the century and a half before New England became the northernmost piece of the United States, the majority of houses were 500 square feet—many, unimaginably, even smaller. When the door (and there was almost always only one door) opened into one of these houses, visitors walked right into the everyday life of the inhabitants. If it was a one-room house, it might have a blanket dividing the room into two parts, but often everything was just right there to be seen.

In such a tiny house, the living, cooking, eating, procreating, birthing, entertaining, dying—all the things that humans do at home—took place there.

Not unusual for its time, the Franklin Smith House, built in Providence sometime before 1828, was 480 square feet, not counting the attic or loft. It's still there, however it appears to have had some work done. In this case, a long shed dormer was added to the back.

The Franklin Smith House in Providence has a small footprint of less than 500 square feet, a size uncommon today except in garages and sheds but quite common in the eighteenth and early nineteenth centuries, when whole families lived in such small structures. Often a loft upstairs served as sleeping quarters for the parents, children, and servants.

"Big House, Little House, Back House, Barn": When Climate Change Meets Economics

Long, rambling buildings assembled themselves over generations and centuries to defeat the frigid climate and to support every phase of farm life.

Thomas C. Hubka is an American architectural historian and professor who admires vernacular architecture. Hubka made an extraordinary discovery for anyone interested in New England's history, economy, and climate.

It is no secret that New England has a shorter growing season than just about anywhere else in the country. It's also been settled by Europeans longer than any other part of North America. As with all invaders of the New World, the first order of the day was survival. That meant staying warm in winter and growing food in summer.

Mother Nature did not smile on the original settlers. The soils are, with few exceptions, rocky; the terrain is hilly. In the seventeenth, eighteenth, and nineteenth centuries, temperatures were far colder than they are today. This worldwide drop in temperatures started in the thirteenth century, invigorated glacier growth, and only began ebbing a century ago.

Let's go back a few hundred years to a rocky and cold New England, where we must build a protective shelter, feed a family, and try not to freeze. That's what the New World meant to those who survived a trip across the Atlantic.

For hearty souls who made it past that first generation, the next couple hundred years meant keeping the growing population alive. Farming and living practices adapted variously to this harsh agricultural climate. One sure way to beat the freeze was to build against it. Which is where Hubka enters.

Facing page: Parts of the Jerathmell Bowers House in Lowell, Massachusetts, which is on the National Register of Historic Places, dates to 1671. It's described as a one-and-a-half story Cape with a central chimney. This was a basic and common form of construction throughout New England. The "cape" refers to Cape Cod–style houses, which are ubiquitous in the Northeast.

Hubka looked at the farm buildings of northern Vermont, New Hampshire, and western Maine and saw a pattern coined by the nursery and jump-rope rhyme that became the title for his 1984 book, *Big House, Little House, Back House, Barn*. His clearheaded deconstruction of all the influences that caused "connected farms" to be built over generations translated common-sense building into a story of how climate and agriculture were resolved in this merciless weather.

Long, rambling buildings assembled themselves over generations and centuries to defeat the frigid climate and to support every phase of

The Lombard Farm in Barnstable, Massachusetts, illustrates the farmer's practical, homegrown method of managing a farm in winter. Instead of trudging through snowbanks (or even heavy rain) to tend the livestock, interlocking structures between outbuildings allow passage from house to barns and other farm work structures without fighting the elements.

farm life. These elongated, evolved strings of structures are located in places other than New England, but Hubka found that the harshest of winters had the greatest impact on architecture's adaptation to climate—especially in New England.

Here, everything froze solid, including oxen, chickens, and grain, unless you covered them with a building. The stench and diseases of farm animals were not welcome inside the home, so barns were built a walking distance away. But when several feet of snow lies on the ground, feeding livestock becomes hazardous duty.

Covered outdoor paths solved the foul weather problem and created sheltered barnyards and work areas that were, in a way, brought

inside. Because buildability was paramount, these rambling work areas that went from house to shed or barn nudged the carpenter's aesthetic sensibility, which required that gables, sheds, and gambrel roof forms were attached to each other, were self-supporting, and would usually do a good job of shedding snow and water. This approach provided a dry and ice-free path between farmhouse and farm buildings.

Architects call telescoping buildings like these "vernacular" structures, in which local materials, familiar technologies, and a style that could adapt to any number of joints, shapes, and surfaces made for an innocently guileless "colonial" aesthetic. When the occupant is the builder and the designer, the results are likely to make sense and fit the site.

Not an actual eighteenth-century farm but an early twentieth-century replica of a house with connecting outbuildings, the Pope Riddle house was designed by the influential New York design firm of McKim, Mead & White. It was built in Farmington, Connecticut, to honor the early American houses that grace the town's historic district.

Hubka realized that the aesthetics were not random and unplanned, but carefully coordinated between raw agricultural needs and the desire for a home to be proud of.

"The idea of balance and unity between house and barn is the most crucial planning idea separating the making of New England connected farmsteads from the previous tradition and from other American farms," Hubka wrote. "New England farmers not only connected their houses to their barns but also broke all traditional farming and building types by applying the architectural detail of the house to the previously unadorned barns."

New England's personality is flinty, one that addresses needs directly, whether building covered bridges, making walls from soil-choking rocks, or combining God and government in meetinghouses. Pretense, affect, and tradition take a backseat to staying alive in a tough place.

Buildings mirror culture and respond to climates. When subsistence farming had to happen during an ice age, "Swamp Yankees" and what they built both worked and created a characteristic New England building.

Imitation in Home Design

Gothic Revival, Italianate, Second Empire, Swiss Chalet, and other fringe nineteenth-century house styles could all be called by-products of success.

Whereas sober practicality was the muse behind the first two hundred years of New England home building, the nineteenth century saw a rising tide of middle-class families not tethered to subsistence farming, occasionally making enough money from an industrializing

The Federal-style Robert S. Burroughs House in Providence, Rhode Island, was built between 1814 and 1817.

The Colton House, on Longmeadow Street in Longmeadow, Massachusetts, was built in 1796 by Captain Gideon Colton.

Built between 1803 and 1805, the Thomas Poynton Ives House has long been considered one of the most elegant homes in Providence. It's been added onto and remodeled over the years. In the 1840s the home was fitted with central heating, plumbing, and gas lighting. Robert H. Ives Goddard Jr. willed the house to Brown University, which owns it still.

The Philips House in Salem, Massachusetts, had an unusual progression to its present state. The house was completed in Danvers, Massachusetts, in 1806, thanks to a wealthy sea captain's daughter Elizabeth Derby, who married Nathaniel West; they divorced shortly after the house was built. However, Elizabeth died in 1814, and when one of her and her ex-husband's daughters died in 1819, Nathaniel inherited a third of the property. He moved four rooms of the house to Salem, where he added more rooms, a hallway, and a third story. The house is now a museum owned by Historic New England.

economy to consider more than subsistence housing. Fantasies could become realities.

These extreme residential caricatures of European antiquities were not only aided by discretionary income and the free time even to think about anything more than the traditional home you were brought up in, but the "picturesque" movement (begun in England) exuded fantasy lives that people could inhabit. An Italianate villa on a hill could harken to Tuscany. A Gothic home could make you feel as though you were in the fourteenth century. Swiss Chalet meant you were in the Alps. Or a Second Empire home could afflict you with a French accent.

These fantasy homes were driven by pattern books, chiefly produced by Andrew Jackson Downing, whose seminal provocative, inspirational 1850 book *The Architecture of Country Houses*, showed chalets, villas, and castles were accessible to average American home builders. This earliest form of "house porn" was often widely built in more open areas of the west, but New England saw inserts of this fanciful bizarreness inserted into any number of cities, towns, and landscapes.

As seen from a different perspective, these hyper-styled homes reflect two classic New England characteristics: personal expression and desire for personal provenance. Despite the desire for puritanical humility, raw self-reliance born of the Calvinist work ethic was the natural by-product of hubris. An architectural fun house announces to the world how you think, what you value, and that you are free to express yourself in your largest, most public possession—your home.

Additionally, New England, while having the deepest roots into its own rocky soil of any part of the United States, was still a land of immigrants, just a few generations removed from the ultimate cultural helicopter parent: old Europe. Like an architectural tattoo, New Englanders could find their own domestic legacy, thank you very much.

The Morse House of Portland, Maine, from 1859, was designed by prolific architect Henry Austin, who created some of New Haven's most unique and elaborate houses as well as Yale's Dwight Hall. He also designed the Egyptian Revival gates of the city's Grove Street Cemetery, the first private, nonprofit cemetery in the world.

The Gothic 1861 Moses Bulkley House at 176 Main Street in Southport, Connecticut, has a fifty-by-fifty-foot cruciform shape and a three-and-a-half-story tower. It was built by architects Lambert and Bunnell.

The 1869 Second Empire–style Pomeroy House built in Southport, Connecticut, by architects Lambert and Bunnell.

Roseland Cottage
Where Presidents Celebrated the Fourth

Its style is called Gothic Revival, and in its heyday in the mid- to late nineteenth century, Henry Bowen's 6,000-square-foot "summer house" in Woodstock, Connecticut, played guest to four presidents—Ulysses Grant, Benjamin Harrison, William McKinley, and Rutherford B. Hayes—as well as welcoming the rich, powerful, and famous.

Non-presidential visitors included abolitionist and Union general John C. Fremont; abolitionist and brother to Harriet, Henry Ward Beecher; and Oliver Wendell Holmes. Its owner, Henry Bowen, made his fortune in newspapers, included among them was *The Independent*, which promoted temperance and abolition.

Besides its immaculately preserved original exterior, which include fancy chimney pots—Gothic Revival architectural detailing—its interior is equally perfectly original, down to the heavily embossed Lincrusta wall covering, furniture, and woodwork.

Roseland today is owned by the nonprofit Historic New England (formerly the Society for the Preservation of New England Antiquities) and is open to the public.

Carpenter Gothic is perfectly manifest in Roseland Cottage, where buildings used wooden takes on the imagery of carved stone in ornament, but whose skin and shape betray a structure that comes from the forests felled to build them.

Stick Style

The same mass-printing revolution in publishing that made Harriet Beecher Stowe's *Uncle Tom's Cabin* and P. T. Barnum's autobiography megahits in the nineteenth century forever changed home design.

In the first half of the nineteenth century, Andrew Jackson Downing was a pioneer in popularizing architectural styles with his two pattern books, *The Architecture of Country Houses* and *Victorian Cottage Residences*. The second half of that century saw many pattern books displaying "Stick style" design, which celebrated the transition to lumber of standard sizes from the heavy post-and-beam construction that had dominated the past two hundred years of New England farm building.

At 76 Bellevue Avenue, at the southeast corner of 36 Old Beach Road in Newport, Rhode Island, is the 1863 John Griswold House, described by the Historic American Buildings Survey as "characterized by open planning, irregular and picturesque massing, deep porches, and richly articulated wall surfaces with bracketing and half-timber patterning."

Architects Edward Tuckerman Potter and Alfred H. Thorp designed this house in Hartford for Mark Twain—or Samuel Clemens—and his family, who resided there for seventeen years beginning in 1874. While living there, Clemens wrote *The Prince and the Pauper*, *The Adventures of Huckleberry Finn*, *The Adventures of Tom Sawyer*, *A Connecticut Yankee in King Arthur's Court*, and other well-known books. Neighbors included Harriet Beecher Stowe and short story writer Bret Harte. Guests would include the best known writers and journalists and actors of their day, including Edwin Booth, brother of John Wilkes Booth.

The new standard-size dimensional lumber was fabricated of thinner, lighter pieces of wood that, in turn, were unified with solid wood sheathing and diagonal bracing. Cumbersome, heavy, and old-fashioned posts and beams were no longer required. The change from a structural post-and-beam frame with perhaps a dozen posts carrying the load of the floors and roof, to a modern house with most loads being carried by continuous bearing walls of smaller, standard-size lumber meant no barn-raisings that required large groups of men. Now homes could be built by a two- or three-man crew, better and faster.

Beyond the technological revolution of mass-produced sawmill lumber replacing hand-hewn posts and beams, the new light-framing technology carried with it a fineness of detailing and decoration not seen before. Color was used in a proto-Victorian manner. In the new mills, wood was patterned into bead board, board and batten, and panelized shingles or clapboards, which could be panelized to make a "woven" exterior as opposed to blank walls perforated by windows and doors. This new structural system was most often balloon framing, where two-story wall studs reached from the ground to the rafters and had floors fastened in between.

From these new production techniques, subsequent Queen Anne detailing and more elaborate shape-shifting could begin the transformation of house design from referencing Europe to becoming fully American. The transition was spearheaded by the New England mentality of Yankee ingenuity triumphing over excuses.

Ultimately, Stick Style was the great-great-grandfather of "platform" framing, where "two-by" dimensional lumber (as in two-by-fours) allowed homes to be affordably built and owned by a massive American middle class that came to exist in the twentieth century. They took the economies of factory-built technology straight into another American invention: the suburbs.

Queen Anne: Victorian "Lite"

In the 1870s, English architect Richard Norman Shaw introduced the Queen Anne or Free Classic style for homes. Although not really derived from any aesthetic of Queen Anne's time in history, the name alluded to the queen of a unified England in the early eighteenth century.

With his fortune from the molasses, sugar, and soap business, Stillman F. Kelley built this elaborate Queen Anne house in Cambridge, Massachusetts, in 1887. After Kelley died in 1911, his wife, Chloe, lived there until her death in 1927, when it was sold to a local junior college.

The style was a hit because it was a nostalgic take on England's elaborate medieval forms. It also appealed to New England home designers who were searching for alternatives to the "same old" colonial and overtly neo-Renaissance and neoclassical fashions of

Architect H. H. Richardson's Watts-Sherman House in Newport, Rhode Island, built in 1874–75.

The Edward S. Dodge House, Cambridge, Massachusetts, built in 1878 by the architectural firm of Longfellow & Clark, is one of many Queen Anne–style houses built in the neighborhood during a time when Cambridge was bursting with well-known personalities. Today the house is on the National Register of Historic Places.

mid-nineteenth-century New England. In truth, this more reserved take on Victorian architecture was a stepping stone to other more distinctively American and New England design sensibilities.

The style's popularity in England meant pattern books offered it up to American designers in accessible illustrations. The first architectural magazine, *The American Architect and Building News*, published Scottish architect Norman Shaw's work, popularizing it in America. It is a style that could easily be applied to the light frame wood construction techniques and American Craftsman-esque detailing that came to dominate home building after the Civil War.

The Watts-Sherman House designed by H. H. Richardson in Newport, Rhode Island, debuted the Queen Anne style in 1875. The focal details and architectural fanciness applied to the designs lent themselves to an industrializing New England, where factory-produced millwork shipped on an ever-growing rail system meant that prefabricated bits of crafty architectural details could be plugged into homes in an expedient manner.

In the early half of the twentieth century, liberation from Queen Anne's symmetry, followed by Shingle style, then Richardson Romanesque, came full circle to Colonial Revival, which made homes no original colonist would have conceived of, beyond materials and details.

Richardsonian Romanesque

Henry Hobson Richardson lived his forty-seven years on this earth in the dead center of the nineteenth century—from 1838 to 1886. He was raised in Louisiana, went to Tulane University, was seduced by Harvard, and was the second American to attend the École des Beaux-Arts in Paris.

He came back to America at the end of the Civil War in 1865 to find himself without work, despite his exceptional credentials and talent. To set himself apart from competitors, he defined a style. He was so successful at creating demand for his particular aesthetic that at the time of his death his name defined it. He had his pick of enviable commissions, most notably Trinity Church Boston, the embodiment of "Richardson Romanesque."

Richardson settled in Medford, Massachusetts, where he and his wife had six children. His commissions were nationwide, but his home was New England.

The name "Romanesque" is a little misleading because it confers a sense that Richardson copied a European affect. Far from it.

His full application of a growing arts and crafts sensibility was truly his own and found its outlet chiefly in houses. These are not Victorian, but ornate; not vernacular, but not untraditional; not Queen Anne, but

Architect Henry Hobson Richardson designed the Thomas Crane Public Library in Quincy, Massachusetts, in 1882. It has been added onto by three subsequent generations of architects: William Martin Aiken in 1908, Paul and Carroll Coletti in 1939, and the firm of Childs Bertman Tseckares Inc., which doubled the size of the library, in 2001.

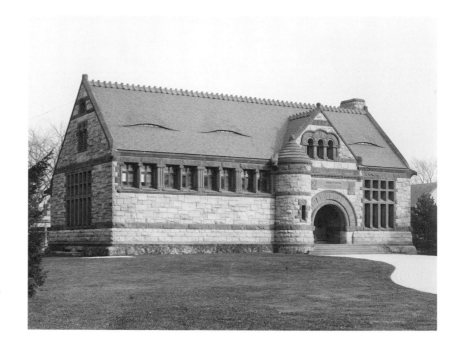

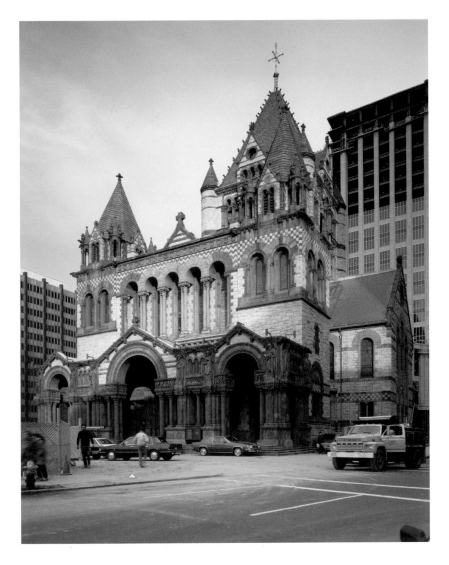

Henry Hobson Richardson won out over five other competitors in a competition to choose the architect for the Trinity Church, on Boston's Copley Square. It's considered by many architecture critics, and even by ordinary people who notice these things, to be H. H. Richardson's best work. Trinity's unique style grew to be revered by the architectural profession, which began to use the term Richardsonian as synonymous for Romanesque architecture.

playing off it. The towers, interweaving ornament, building shape, and expressive detailing of Richardson Romanesque created a unique style that survived his short life.

ACCEPTED·DESIGN·FOR
CAMBRIDGE·CITY·HALL

Longfellow, Alden & Harlow.
Architects

Today home of the first legal application for same-sex marriage in 2004 (granted), the Cambridge City Hall was designed by the architectural firm of Longfellow, Alden & Harlow, who oversaw its construction in 1888–1889.

The creative spark of Richardson was both fresh and had gravitas to a new generation of American industrialist patrons.

According to biographer James F. O'Gorman, Richardson's "reckless disregard for financial order" meant that he died in debt and left nearly nothing to his family—a wife and six children.

The handsome Boston Water
Works complex and Roxbury
standpipe, both built in the
mid-nineteenth century.

Robert H. Robertson, a New York architect,
designed the Pequot Library in Southport,
Connecticut, in 1885–1887 and built it over
six years beginning in 1887. He and his
former partner, William Potter, had designed
Gothic church buildings in New York City
that showed the influence of architect
Henry Hobson Richardson; Richardsonian
Romanesque also characterizes the Pequot.

Court Street
Pretty Little Houses All in a Row

If you know New Haven, you know Wooster Square, the intimate counterpart to the very public New Haven green. Wooster Square is primarily surrounded by homes, mostly from the nineteenth century, some of which represent the most beautiful architecture New Haven has to offer—from row houses or freestanding Italianate "villas."

But there is a less well-known but equally compelling section of the Wooster Square District that is, on some levels, exquisitely "perfect"—Court Street. Court Street is a classic narrow urban street flanked by row houses, all built either at the same time or very close to it in lockstep visual coordination. It has undergone a series of changes that mirror the ebbs and flows of differing economies, visions of what houses should be, and finally how urban centers like New Haven can find a future where people begin to reoccupy our cities.

The majority of Court Street was built by the Home Insurance Company in 1870. It was a spectacular failure, and the buildings were sold for $7,500 each by the probate court—and, fittingly enough, that is the source of the street's name.

What makes all row houses compelling is their repetitively residential nature with stair-accessed stoops and small-scale detailing. This effect is even more pronounced on Court Street, where,

because one developer created the vast majority of homes, there is a consistency that allows trees, individual door colors and other pertinences and appointments that can have enhanced meaning, which is true of all row-house renovations.

As built in 1870, the row houses themselves typically had four floors, plus a basement, and the lowest floor, typically where kitchens and servants would live, was accessed by walking down a half level. Up the front steps would be the parlor and dining areas, with bedrooms on the top two floors above that.

Essentially, the Court Street townhouses were all twenty feet wide and thirty feet deep—quite small. And in fact, when built, not only were they economically unfeasible but also they were greatly behind the curve for luxury housing because those who could afford the asking price for these well-built residences were moving elsewhere for freestanding homes.

Sadly, the vast majority of these row houses were subdivided into rooming houses into the 1920s, and from well-kept rooming houses, this neighborhood devolved into a virtual "skid row" until 1960, when New Haven's penchant for urban renewal caught up with this little neighborhood's devolved state.

The City opted to encourage private redevelopment of these row houses into single-family or floor-by-floor apartment conversions (versus tenement rooming houses). The street was narrowed to a single one-way lane, with access limited to those who lived on it, and the classic 1960s and '70s tree planters, benches, and so on soon created a vision of urban re-inhabitation and gentrification that did more than stabilize the sad state of this block. The saving of Court Street was so successful that the original diverse group of tenants and owners has evolved into a new generation of homeowners rehabbing the rehabs that were done in the 1960s.

Shingle Style: As American as New England

Here, shown during its mere seventy-five years of existence, is the William Low House in Bristol, Rhode Island, the epitome of Shingle style that was designed and built by McKim, Mead & White in 1887. Today we can only appreciate the photographs of this classic structure, because it was demolished in 1962.

Toward the end of the nineteenth and beginning of the twentieth centuries, American architects were feeling their oats. In Chicago and the Midwest, a group that included Louis Sullivan and Frank Lloyd Wright were creating a completely American aesthetic, reinventing the nature of buildings with steel, large plate-glass windows, and botanic ornamentation.

All this was happening with a blind eye to Europe, whose buildings had forever before been the model of what was built here. Architecture schools sprang up all across the country, including four in Boston alone.

The Malvern Hotel, Bar Harbor, Mount Desert Island, Maine, was built in 1912 and—along with a half-dozen other luxury hotels—burned to ashes in the fall of 1947. The lovely Shingle-style hotel wasn't alone; "the Year Maine Burned," as it was called, consumed 851 homes, nearly 400 seasonal cottages, nine towns, and a quarter-million acres of land, including half of Acadia National Park.

The overwrought and imitative pandering of architects to a Eurocentric standard was rejected by this generation of American architects. America was finding its own distinct cultural voice—nothing new for New England, which was founded three hundred years earlier on the principle of cultural rejection.

It was only natural that creative New England architects would find a method that was anything but European and run with it. The Shingle Style had a host of origins and expressions that created a singularly distinctive form of architecture. At once asymmetric, with a strictly limited palette of materials, this "style" celebrated the joys of wood framing that the forests of the New World bountifully provided.

It was a spontaneous hybrid of Queen Anne porches and wood-shingled surfaces, asymmetrical forms with Colonial Revival roofs, columns, Palladian windows, and preplanned elements that were intended to seem to be additions. The Shingle style used the shapes of Richardsonian Romanesque, though rendered in wood. It also used

The elaborately shingled Mary Fiske-Stoughton House in Cambridge, Massachusetts, was designed by H. H. Richardson and built in 1883. The house became a National Historic Landmark in 1989.

Richardsonian Romanesque's fieldstone foundations and chimneys as a counterpoint to the sea of shingle shapes. These complex shapes were gift-wrapped with uniform wood shingle surfaces that clarity of materials gave order to its ad hoc complexities. H. H. Richardson and William Ralph Emerson of Boston, and John Calvin Stevens of Portland, Maine, led the New England architects in Shingle style design, but a slew of New York architects found the New England landscape a perfect situation for Shingle-style homes.

Its essential adaptability was reincarnated when brilliant Yale architectural historian Vincent Scully noted in his seminal 1974 book, *The Shingle Style Today*, that a new generation of mid-twentieth-century architects were, knowingly or not, seizing upon the same sense of spontaneous architectural combustion to create houses, many in New England, that once again rejected a dominant European architectural paradigm, this time Modernism.

In 1881 Edwin J. Hulbert built (and possibly even designed) a beachside Shingle-style house in Nantucket, Massachusetts, which he named Sandanwede. The house was an early vacation house on Nantucket, which is today more known for vacation houses than anything else.

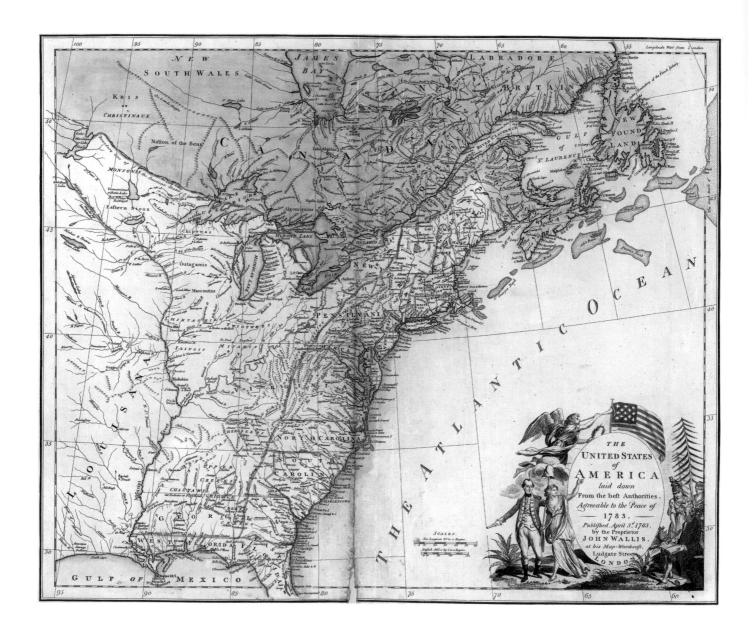

THE
UNITED STATES
of
AMERICA
laid down
From the best Authorities,
Agreeable to the Peace of
1783.
Published April 3.ᵈ 1783,
by the Proprietor
JOHN WALLIS,
at his Map-Warehouse,
Ludgate Street,
LONDON.

Through War to Independence

4

By the mid-1700s the American colonies, especially the New England colonies, had lost all faith in England. Elsewhere, those who paid attention to the relationship saw a great split looming and knew it would be violent.

For Great Britain, its New World colony was of immense strategic and economic importance, both for its lavish natural resources and as a seat of operations to reach into the North American continent. With its American colonies as the base, England could rapidly deploy whenever necessary and expand its dominant military influence still farther.

Yet as the colonies grew and as time passed and its citizens increasingly were born and grew up in the colonies, a new culture called America emerged. Patriot attachment to Great Britain faded. The northern colonies came to call themselves New England, and whatever they achieved, in whatever type of house they lived, eating whatever they grew, and with whatever local government they had—they did it on their own, and it was theirs.

England was unwilling to let go. The colonies chafed and became outraged with distant England's incessant and ever-increasing demand for more—more resources, money, and blind obedience.

Facing page: Thirteen states, not colonies, in the hard-won union are shown in part of a 1783 map. Washington, shown beside a woman believed to be Liberty, stands under the angel of peace, who blows her trumpet beneath the flag of the United States with its thirteen stars. Canada is to the north, and out west looms a gigantic Louisiana.

His Highness Overtaxes His Subjects

Painted here in his coronation robes, George III served as king of England from 1760 to 1820.

By the mid-eighteenth century, the Crown had installed a growing list of taxes on every imaginable luxury and commodity to help finance the continued unwanted presence of British soldiers and sailors in America. They were stationed to protect the king's investment against Indians and especially against the French, to expand and defend its dominant commerce, and to mobilize for military problems that erupted in the North Atlantic.

Increasingly, Americans weren't shy about condemning the cost. This disapproval of His Majesty's government was perceived as ungratefulness. England had provided them with expensive security, an investment that allowed the colonies to exist in the first place and that created the continuing safety the colonies required to prosper and grow. Like all investors, England expected its investment in North America to pay off.

The colonies, meanwhile, had visibly and measurably grown and prospered. From a population of three thousand in 1630, their numbers increased to fourteen thousand in 1640, sixty-eight thousand in 1680, and close to one hundred thousand by 1700. By the time of the Revolution, New England was home to nearly one million citizens, and many (if not most) felt a greater attachment to this homeland and to their homegrown leaders than they did to England and to his most sacred majesty, George III, king of Great Britain.

Weary of Paying the King's Protection Money

Colonial attitudes had not soured overnight about the British, who had always taken a paternal, if not superior, attitude toward the colonies. The British were constantly hungry for money and could be extremely demanding about it. Yet the thousands of trained and equipped British soldiers expensively outfitted and shipped for a posting in America were admittedly helpful for defense against the Indians and the French.

The less dependent on British help the colonials became, and the less they felt threatened by the Indians or the French (or the more they felt capable of defending themselves against either), the greater grew their discontent over what they saw as a British occupation and the burdensome taxation that enabled it.

Although they were still British subjects, the idea of breaking away began simmering, first in whispers and quiet conversations, then openly and brazenly.

Among the unfolding acts of Parliament that seemed to move the colonists further toward independence were the Molasses Act of 1733 and the Sugar Act of 1764, both of which increased taxes on necessary sweets from the West Indies, which colonists were not allowed to import for themselves because of a British blockade.

Parliament then passed the second Currency Act in 1764 because, as His Majesty's government stated, colonial currency was dragging down the value of the British pound. Therefore, colonists were prohibited henceforth from issuing their own money.

From today's perspective, probably worst of all was the Quartering Act of 1765, which required colonists to house and feed a British soldier if so ordered. Even in today's world of over-spacious houses with

Facing page: Engraver Paul
Revere made this illustration
of what came to be known as
the Boston Massacre, which
occurred on Boston's King
Street on March 5, 1770, when
British soldiers fired on a
group that had gathered to
harass them. Without orders,
and likely feeling threatened,
the soldiers shot into the
crowd, killing five men and
injuring several others.

guest bedrooms and sizable mother-in-law suites, providing room and board for a soldier would be a burdensome annoyance.

Imagine what an immense inconvenience it would have been for a New England family to house an additional adult, given that the average eighteenth-century American house was often smaller than a modern two-car garage. When you see existing houses from the eighteenth century, you rarely see the original small structures. Over the years these have been torn down or remodeled and added onto to such an extent that they're hardly recognizable for what they were.

The Stamp Act, which was enacted in 1765 to boost funding for the British, imposed a tax on nearly everything made of paper, from marriage licenses to newspapers, deeds, playing cards, licenses, birth certificates, and death certificates. Anything official that was printed on paper was required to bear an embossed revenue stamp, showing that the required tax had been paid.

There followed various others of what were called "inflammatory" acts, all of which seemed like punishment to the people of New England, who, in Boston one day in March 1770, congealed into the form of a mob that had taken from the British all they were prepared to take.

They began throwing sticks and stones at a squad of British soldiers, who responded with musket fire, killing five colonists and wounding several others.

The next of the inflammatory acts was the 1773 Tea Act, which gave the nearly bankrupt British East India Company an intentional government-assisted boost with a monopoly on the sale of tea in the colonies. In response, this was followed in 1773 by the Boston Tea Party, in which tons of British tea were thrown into Boston Harbor by Bostonians dressed as Indians.

The BLOODY MASSACRE perpetrated in King-∫ Street BOSTON on March 5th 1770 by a party of the 29th REGT.

Engrav'd Printed & Sold by PAUL REVERE BOSTON

BUTCHER'S HALL

Unhappy BOSTON! see thy Sons deplore,
Thy hallow'd Walks besmear'd with guiltless Gore:
While faithless P—n and his savage Bands,
With murd'rous Rancour stretch their bloody Hands;
Like fierce Barbarians grinning o'er their Prey,
Approve the Carnage, and enjoy the Day.

If scalding drops from Rage from Anguish Wrung
If speechless Sorrows lab'ring for a Tongue
Or if a weeping World can ought appease
The plaintive Ghosts of Victims such as these;
The Patriot's copious Tears for each are shed,
A glorious Tribute which embalms the Dead.

But know, FATE summons to that awful Goal,
Where JUSTICE strips the Murd'rer of his Soul:
Should venal C—ts the scandal of the Land,
Snatch the relentless Villain from her Hand,
Keen Execrations on this Plate inscrib'd,
Shall reach a JUDGE who never can be brib'd.

The unhappy Sufferers were Mess.rs SAM.L GRAY, SAM.L MAVERICK, JAM.S CALDWELL, CRISPUS ATTUCKS & PAT.K CARR
Killed. Six wounded; two of them (CHRIST.R MONK & JOHN CLARK) Mortally
Published in 1770 by Paul Revere Boston

England's prime minister, Lord North, told Parliament that the "Americans have tarred and feathered your subjects, plundered your merchants, burnt your ships, denied all obedience to your laws and authority; yet so clement and so long forbearing has our conduct been that it is incumbent on us now to take a different course. Whatever may be the consequences, we must risk something; if we do not, all is over."

What North had in mind was eventually dubbed by the colonists as the "Intolerable Acts." These took several forms.

First the British closed the port of Boston, which was a big deal for the second largest port in North America. Only Philadelphia's was larger, with New York and Charleston, South Carolina, bringing up third and fourth.

Next the British employed the Administration of Justice Act, which required that any officer of the king (e.g., soldier, sailor, ship captain,

The able Doctor, or America Swallowing the Bitter Draught.

Subtle it's not, but the cartoon that shows tea being poured down America's throat (the reclined woman) helped further inflame American sentiments against what were termed the Intolerable Acts, which closed the port of Boston, allowed British troops to be quartered in the colonies, allowed British officers to be tried in friendly English courts for offenses in America, and all but eliminated self-government in Massachusetts.

bureaucrat) accused of a crime in the colonies could stand trial only in England. Any American witness testifying against the king's officer must travel to England for the trial, paying his own way to England and back while remaining there as long as he was needed to testify and paying all his own expenses while there. Of course, while there, the colonist would be without a source of income, because his livelihood was back home in North America.

This clearly was a case of punishment, not justice.

Next, in something called the Massachusetts Government Act, the British took control of the government of New England's largest state. This outrage was quickly followed by a revised version of the Quartering Act.

Fundamentally, the British were going all in on the Boston insurgency with a message that said, "We're in charge, and you'll do what we tell you to do."

After that, it went downhill fast in the relationship between king and colony. Before long, Patrick Henry was choosing between liberty or death, followed toe-to-heel by the minutemen, Paul Revere, and Bunker Hill.

A Revolution by Degrees

For a lot of reasons, the British were reluctant for war with their thirteen North American colonies.

How would they possibly patrol and control the one thousand miles of coastline from Maine to Savannah? Although they would be taking on a poorly outfitted but tenacious force, how might England successfully prosecute a war in an area that was ten times the size of England?

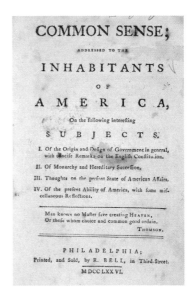

In 1776 Thomas Paine published his revolutionary pamphlet *Common Sense* for American audiences. Its subjects were "the Origin and Design of Government in general, with concise Remarks on the English Constitution;" "Of Monarchy and Hereditary Succession;" "Thoughts on the present State of American Affairs;" and "Of the present Ability of America, with some miscellaneous Reflections." The sum of the pamphlet was to push colonists to revolt against England.

Sited beside the Old North Bridge in Concord, Massachusetts, Daniel Chester French's *Minute Man* monument is on the spot where the first American fell during the start of the American Revolution. LIBRARY OF CONGRESS, PHOTOGRAPH BY CAROL HIGHSMITH.

The colonists soon provided what the king and his ministers needed to proceed.

Officially, "the shot heard 'round the world" began the Revolution on April 18, 1775, at Concord, Massachusetts. But all the recent history, conflicts, taxes, retributive acts by the king, along with the passive, subtle, then outright resistance to British rule by colonists, all led to insurrection, long before that famous shot had coalesced the colonies into an organized and growing defiance.

After almost 150 years of existence, the colonies had grown to believe that England was no longer their country, that the new American continent was their home, and that what they made of it should be their decision alone. At this point, these stubborn and self-sufficient colonists could make do without much of the "help" the British provided and certainly could put to better use the money they were paying England for unwanted soldiers, bureaucrats, and tax collectors.

This realization was not limited to Boston or New England, although the anger and violence first reached its boiling point there. While half of New Yorkers were part of the 20 percent of New World residents who called themselves "Loyalists," New Englanders overwhelmingly opposed the Crown and supported self-governance.

In Boston on March 5, 1770, the king's soldiers killed five male colonists and injured six others. The perception of the Crown was never the same. Among others, Paul Revere and Samuel Adams recognized a breaking point between a profitable, free New England and its profligate absentee owner. Ironically, John Adams, later an American president, defended the British soldiers in court, putting the rule of law above personal opinions.

No matter the cause, the act of killing protestors made England a threatening foreign power for New Englanders, and soon after for the rest of the colonies. Wars start and then end things. In New England the rejection of Mother England in the name of religious expression became wholesale political divorce when five men died in Boston.

The split was now more than theological. The all-consuming revolution meant some fled to the safety of fealty in Canada. What remained became distilled and purified in the hotbed of freedom that New England championed.

Since the Boston Massacre, New England's major strengths—shipping and commerce—suffered more from the British than from competition from Philadelphia and New York. Ironically, law forced the descendants of those who fled British religious intolerance to trade only with the mother country. But even the law and its potential punishments did not stop New Englanders from trading with the enemy—France.

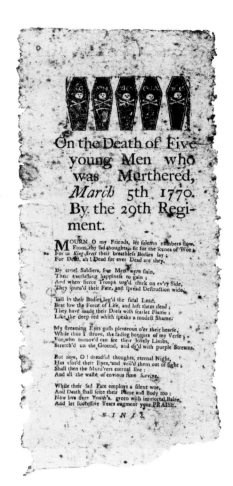

A pamphlet from 1770, *On the Death of Five Young Men Who Was Murthered, March 5th, 1770. By the 29th Regiment*, **a regiment of the British army.**

Paul Revere

Paul Revere was not descended from Pilgrims. His father sailed from France to North America, where he became a craftsman. Paul was named after his father Apollos, who had previously changed the family name from Rivoire.

Of course Revere was immortalized after the 1861 Henry Wadsworth Longfellow poem that bore his name:

> *Listen my children and you shall hear*
> *Of the midnight ride of Paul Revere,*
> *On the eighteenth of April, in Seventy-five;*
> *Hardly a man is now alive*
> *Who remembers that famous day and year.*

Although the poem was filled with the poet's license to re-create facts in favor of literary impact, Revere was an extraordinary example of Boston's seminal role in fomenting revolution in the colonies. He was a classic Boston native, silversmith, engraver, and, yes, dentist, who as a boy made extra money ringing the church bells at Old North Church.

While he grew to be quite successful using his many talents, he saw the money-grubbing Crown as potentially wrecking his livelihood and the freedoms colonists had come to enjoy.

Revere had none of the religious zealotry or agrarian history in his lineage. He was of French Huguenot background. A craftsman from the age of twelve, he had to take over the family business at nineteen when his father died. He joined the British army in America in 1754 to fight the French at Lake George, New York. Back home he joined the Freemasons; got to know Samuel Adams, James Otis, and John Hancock; and joined a litany of insurgent organizations—the Boston Committee of Safety, the Massachusetts Committee of Safety, Boston Committee of Correspondence, Sons of Liberty, North End Caucus, and the North End Caucus—all devoted to political opposition. During the decade before his famous ride, the Sugar, Stamp, and Townsend Acts help nurture his anti-British sentiments and led to his participation in the Boston Tea Party. He memorialized the Boston Massacre in an interpretive drawing and became a rider for the Whig Patriots.

Revere ran messages between various other members of the emerging revolution while spying on British troop movements. Yet it's uncertain how well he would be remembered today if it weren't for Longfellow. Revere's ride was what captured the poet's imagination and forever drilled "one if by land, two if by sea" into the brains of every American schoolchild.

The poem, however, never mentions an event that occurred a few years later. Revere the soldier was court-martialed but not convicted of cowardice and incompetence when he commanded the artillery for army general Solomon Lovell, whose inaction lost a 1779 battle to capture a coastal fort the British were building in Maine.

His life after the Revolutionary War fully reveled in its success: He created the plates from which the first Continental currency was printed and designed the first state seal of Massachusetts and the seal for the new United States. He was a county coroner, the president of the Boston Board of Health, and cofounded a fire insurance company.

The post-war freedoms Revere helped secure enabled him to aggressively expand his businesses to include a copper mill, a forge, and a foundry for casting bells and cannons. Meanwhile, he continued his lifelong artisanship in silversmithing. His rich life was further enriched with sixteen children from two wives and more than fifty grandchildren before his death in 1818 at the age of eighty-three.

The Paul Revere House, 19 North Square, Boston, in a 1941 photograph.

A printed message from the Sons of Liberty, an underground group that grew up within the thirteen colonies to fight the onerous taxes and other oppressions they felt the British were forcing on them.

By *the* LION *&* UNICORN, Dieu & mon droit, *their Lieutenant-Generals, Governours, Vice Admirals, &c. &c. &c. &c.*

A HUE *&* CRY.

WHEREAS I have been informed, from undoubted authority, that a certain PATRICK HENRY, of the county of Hanover, and a number of *deluded followers*, have taken up arms, chosen their officers, and, styling themselves an *independent company*, have marched out of their county, encamped, and put themselves in a posture of war; and have written and despatched letters to divers parts of the country, exciting the people to join in these *outrageous* and *rebellious* practices, to the *great terrour* of all his Majesty's *faithful* subjects, and in *open defiance* of *law* and *government* ; and have *committed* other *acts of violence*, particularly in *extorting* from his Majesty's *Receiver-General* the sum of 330 l. under *pretence* of *replacing the powder* I *thought proper* to order from the magazine; whence it undeniably appears, there is *no longer* the least security for the *life* or *property* of any man: Wherefore, I have *thought proper, with the advice of his Majesty's Council*, and *in his Majesty's name*, to issue this *my* proclamation, strictly charging *all persons*, upon their *allegiance*, not to *aid, abet*, or *give countenance* to the said PATRICK HENRY, *or any other persons* concerned in *such unwarrantable combinations;* but, on the contrary, to oppose *them*, and *their designs*, by *every means,* which designs must otherwise inevitably involve the *whole country* in the *most direful calamity*, as they will call for the *vengeance of offended Majesty*, and the *insulted laws*, to be *exerted here*, to vindicate the *constitutional* authority of government.

Given, *&c. this 6th day of May,* 1775.

D****.

G * * d * * * the P * * * *.

The packet boat *Hannah* out of Rhode Island was one of the boats used to smuggle goods into the colonies. One day a British schooner belonging to the Custom Service, the HMS *Gaspee*, was chasing the *Hannah* and ran aground near Warwick, Rhode Island. Although it could have floated free when the tide came in, the captain did not get the chance to sail away. Members of the Sons of Liberty attacked, ransacked the ship, and set it afire.

The Sons of Liberty had formed in 1765 as an underground group to foment full-on revolution sufficient to make Boston the first liberated American city in 1776.

Organizing for Revolution

Before and during the Revolution, all able-bodied men were required to serve in the militia. During the French and Indian Wars, the colonial militia fought alongside the British.

Militia members were farmers, tradesmen, and professionals who trained and drilled on a sometimes-regular basis. In the years just before the Revolution, another group arose. These were the minutemen, a colonial "Special Forces" who were the Green Berets, SEALS, and SWAT operatives of their time.

The minutemen (Paul Revere was a member) trained for rapid deployment, hence the name. Members had to be thirty years old or younger. These were the fastest, strongest members of the colonial militia. Like most men of their time, they were already familiar with fighting. The frontier tactics that colonists learned during the French and Indian Wars proved invaluable against the British, who apparently had not learned those same lessons.

The type of fighting the minutemen practiced is what the military now calls "irregular warfare." Unlike most members of the militia, the minutemen didn't fall into ranks with other soldiers but instead hid in brush and fields and trees and hills and fired on the enemy strategically and unpredictably.

Throughout the war the minutemen proved to be an extremely valuable force and often caught the British by surprise—even during battles with the colonial militia.

Picture the scene: the well-equipped, experienced, and highly trained British army, moving straight toward the colonial army, marching in close ranks, and wearing highly visible red coats. Unseen and off to the side were men dressed to blend into the North American

Noah Webster
An American Savant

Despite being descendants of Connecticut and Massachusetts governors, Noah Webster's family was from West Hartford, Connecticut, where they farmed barely enough food to feed themselves and earned a little extra money as weavers. Everyone pitched in at the family farm, and Noah's four siblings did not attend school at all. When Noah was born in 1758, he clearly was an unusual child.

But Webster's parents immediately knew Noah had a rare intellect that needed feeding, and they used every penny they had to give him a full grammar school education and four years at Yale. When Noah wanted to go on to law school, his father confessed that he had no more money to support him, and Noah paid his way by teaching.

It might well be that Noah Webster was a highly functional savant, as his life was filled with extreme precision and application of organization. He counted every house in New York City; was obsessed with disease and epidemics; was passionate about words, language, and education's failings; and acted, intensely, to make his fascinations useful in a way that uniquely focused on a distinct American sensibility.

Having taught, Webster knew students needed guidance, and he wrote the so-called *Blue Back Speller* in 1783, a book that was used for over a century and sold 100 million copies.

Noah Webster

Noah Webster, who gave birth to proper spelling and the modern dictionary, was born in this 1750 house in West Hartford, Connecticut. He died in New Haven in 1843 and is buried in that city's Grove Street Cemetery.

Before the seventeenth century, dictionaries were largely limited to Latin and Greek. A small English dictionary was published in 1604, but in 1801 Webster saw the need for a distinctly American dictionary—it took him twenty-seven years, but, at age seventy, he published an American dictionary with sixty-five-thousand words. Cultures use language to define and express themselves; Webster's dictionary was a huge definition of a people quite distinct from their English ancestors that served to give the United States a mirror of its distinction and a vehicle for its expression.

His focus was unrelenting but broad: He was passionate about a strong federal government,

disliked the Bill of Rights, wanted women to have educational opportunity—but only in homemaking. He thought no one should vote before they were forty-five and no one should hold office until they were fifty. He offered up a new translation of the Bible that eliminated the "dirty" parts and supported the idea of a state church in Connecticut.

By all accounts he was a good father to his eight children, was deeply devoted to his wife, and had a classic Great Awakening religious conversion at her facilitation in 1808. Despite that and his conservative views, he reveled in convivial socializing with party animal Ben Franklin.

wilderness, skilled in the art of hunting, familiar with the land and the people who lived on it, and highly motivated to protect their new country.

Who would you put your money on?

Takes Root in New England, Blossoms in Pennsylvania

When you hear the name Ben Franklin you automatically think of the word Philadelphia. Yet Franklin's life began in 1706 in Boston, where his unique character of renegade genius was first established and set for life.

He was baptized in 1706 at Old South Church and entered Boston Grammar School at eight because his father, Josiah, wanted him to become a preacher. Money was tight, though, and his formal education ended after two years. His informal education never stopped.

Franklin's intense love of reading allowed him to absorb knowledge wherever he happened to be. First he worked in his father's soap- and candle-making business. But soon he found the prime setting for his verbal obsession by working at his older brother James's print shop.

The young Franklin was as free a thinker as he was a bookworm, and he soon began writing, advocated vegetarianism, invented swim fins, published and sold ballads, and was generally unrelenting in his desire to learn, experiment, and innovate. Things got very interesting when the brothers Franklin decided to publish a newspaper called the *New-England Courant.* Never content to simply earn a living, Franklin started writing into the paper under the pseudonym Mrs. Silence

The famous 1785 portrait of polymath Benjamin Franklin, painted by Joseph Duplessis.

Benjamin Franklin in London at the Court of St. James.

Dogood. Mrs. Dogood's fourteen letters to the paper were explosively popular with everybody except brother James. (Franklin later wrote under the names Polly Baker and Richard Saunders.)

The fraternal disagreement reached the point when, at age sixteen, Ben broke his apprenticeship indenture and fled first to New York then to his adopted hometown of Philadelphia. It was there that he started eating meat and growing into the man we have all studied from kindergarten on.

It was also there that Franklin began a succession of intellectual, scientific, and journalistic triumphs that make him one of the planet's most interesting occupants in any era.

In Philadelphia he opened his own printing shop, created the concept of a lending library, started a volunteer fire brigade, helped found the University of Pennsylvania and a hospital, published *Poor Richard's Almanac* for the next twenty-five years, learned four languages, and created the American Philosophical Society—all before turning forty.

Franklin then did groundbreaking work in experimentation with electricity, created the Franklin Stove and the urinary catheter, conceived the principle of evaporative refrigeration, and invented bifocal glasses. Franklin attended the Boston Latin School as a child. As an adult he was elected to the State Assembly, became the first US postmaster general, and got degrees from Harvard, Yale, and Oxford while, after a generous contribution, helped to found what became Franklin & Marshall College. With his intellect and curiosity, all the formal education Franklin needed he got in two years of grammar school.

His unending inspiration and service in creating America from the British colonies is legendary, especially in charming the French into active support for the Revolution. His central role is reflected by his signature on four of the country's formative documents: the Declaration of Independence, the Treaty of Alliance with France, the Treaty of Paris that ended the Revolutionary War, and the US Constitution.

Franklin died at age eighty-four, fully embraced in the bosom of Pennsylvania and Philadelphia, but truly a son of New England.

Exporting New England to the Midwest

In the nineteenth century, new settlements to the west revealed that there was an expansive country that had once been under an enormous inland sea (what is now the prairie) where twenty to thirty inches of beautiful rock-free, arable soil was available just by busting up the sod that covered it. Many left New England for the Midwestern and prairie states. Many New England farmers stayed put, replacing crops with pastures and livestock.

Ultimately, even that proved to be scarcely tenable, and eventually the majority of farms that once denuded the forestland of New England gave up the ghost. People either moved to cities to work in factories, or they went west to start farms, leaving those mute rock walls where they stood.

What remains today is the image of relatively young forests completely engulfing stone walls. The insatiable natural growth is utterly ignorant of the millions of hours of backbreaking human labor needed to move the stones, create walls, and farm the land. The poignancy is undeniable. A herculean effort proved futile, and the bottomless reservoir of life force that is our natural world swallowed what humankind had only temporarily conquered.

Ribbons of Rock

One of Robert M. Thorson's great books on New England's stone walls has a beautiful description of "ribbons of rock" silently racing through the countryside. Thorson cites a 1939 estimate—made by mining engineer Oliver Bowles from an 1872 Department of Agriculture report on fences—that there were 240,000 miles of walls crisscrossing the New England landscape, longer than the entire coastline of the United States.

People find the stone walls beautiful as well as heavy stacks of information: An active group of "stone wall tourists" seeks out these now-useless barriers, combining disciplines of history, geology, topography, and hiking to retrace the archeology of a bygone agricultural era.

Crashing into a New World nearly four centuries ago, European settlers had to learn to feed themselves. Survival meant taming New England's rolling hills and farming its rocky soil.

Glaciers rolled millions upon millions of rocks across thousands of miles of landscape, crushing them deep into the ground as they went along, finally dropping off their lightest till to create Long Island.

When European settlers encountered hillsides packed with rocks (along with old-growth trees), the only option was for these desperate-but-dogged land tamers to remove the rocks from the soil, one at a time, and assemble the rocks into boundary lines between properties or between sections of larger farms. If the settler was fortunate, there might be an ox or two available to lend muscle to the stone-removal effort, but mostly it was human backs that were broken in the endless struggle to undo thousands of years of natural force.

Whether they are (as Thorson classifies them) "rectangular stack," "inward-slanted, battered," or "triangular-form fieldstone fences," stone walls were not merely products of farmers defining their fields.

From Puritans to Patriots: An American Evolution

The American sense of cultural freedom—freedoms now enshrined in the Constitution—was not limited to New England, but it was in New England that rejection of British dominance was woven into the culture. The original Puritans had long faded away or been assimilated by the less pious. Still, the power of the New England pulpit remained undiminished.

James Davenport, namesake of Yale's Davenport College, was a strict Puritan minister who came from a wealthy British family, and his mother was descended from royalty. Yet he was also a part of the mid-eighteenth-century's Great Awakening, a religious rejection of traditional English norms of class and privilege, including the idea that freedom of speech was a gift from God.

So the piety of the Puritans tempered, and the religious evolution mirrored the colonies' conflicted civil life as New England's Congregational Church split into Old Light and New Light factions. New denominations also arose, such as the Baptist church, which attracted new members. The Great Awakening condemned the Anglican religious hierarchy and preached a theology of personal responsibility to God that defines religious expression as a human right versus a governmental obligation—an early separation of church and state.

In pulpits, farms, and cities, anger at the Crown grew into insurrection. The loudest voices of rejection of the king's impositions were found in New England, despite it being a place that disproportionally benefited from the British navy's protection of shipping routes. Having thirteen separate governments and a variety of disparate cultures

Milestones
Finding Our Way

When people had to walk or ride a horse from place to place, even a journey through little New England could get complicated if you were traveling new ground. Roads were often built atop old Indian routes, which more or less were worn paths.

As roads began being built with more planning and intention, they linked town to town, and smaller roads led off to a big farm or to a quarry or some other destination.

In the late seventeenth century, determined individuals began finding, chiseling, and erecting

Milestone, 741 Canton Avenue, Milton, Norfolk County, Massachusetts.

Bay Road, Wenham, Essex County, Massachusetts.

All three above: Great Road and Old Ayer Road, Groton, Middlesex County, Massachusetts.

Below Left: Main and Foster Streets, Melrose, Middlesex County, Massachusetts. Center: East end of town common, West Brookfield, Worcester County, Massachusetts. Right: Route 9, Leicester, Worcester County, Massachusetts.

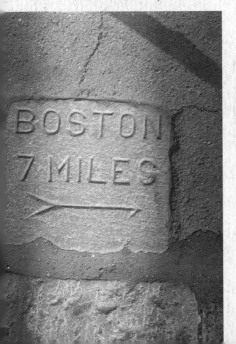

The two types of milestones were for highway travelers and turnpike travelers. Today these terms have slightly different—if not opposite—meanings. The colonists' "highways" were the most commonly traveled routes, and they began in the seventeenth and eighteenth centuries following old Indian trails. Turnpikes were thought-out, planned transportation routes and usually were straighter.

Public Alley No. 102, near Marshall Street, Boston, Suffolk County, Massachusetts.

location markers that became known as milestones. These would keep travelers up on how far they had come and how far they had to go. Many of these were on roads that led to Boston. Others went to smaller towns and villages. All milestones had both destination and distance in Roman numerals chiseled into the stone.

With this information, people could gauge progress, try to time an overnight stay at a village or farm, assess whether there was enough food to go much farther, and overall have a better sense of when they would arrive at their destination.

Worcester Turnpike, Westborough, Worcester County, Massachusetts.

within them come together and agree (despite profound differences) to fight the world's largest and most dominant military power for the freedom to make their own decisions was an extreme act of defiance and of faith.

New England's Revolutionary War costs were not limited to the over 100,000 who died either fighting or because of disease and imprisonment (evenly split between American and British). War puts much of life on hold, as eight years of seesaw insurrection, retaliation, and battle burned both literal and symbolic bridges between the mother country and its rebellious namesake.

But the dramatic eighteenth-century revolutions in New England, along with religion, education, technology, and governance, had an abiding, and expanding basis: agriculture. At the end of the Revolutionary War, farming was still the economic basis for survival in almost every household.

Farms needed at least fifty acres to sustain a family, but it was hard for an eighteenth-century family to manage more than three hundred acres. Almost all farms had livestock. If you did not own land, you rented acreage, and if you could not rent, you were hired to work on another family's farm. Households were largely self-sufficient, but not all were growing food. Craftsmen made furniture, barrels, and pots, while other occupations included blacksmiths, preachers, and doctors.

A Time of Abundance

As cities grew, tradesmen marketed imported and processed commodities like spices, cloth, hardware, and crockery. Farms grew, and technologies became more proficient, as seeds, husbandry, and planting

Constructed in the late 1820s, the Dexter Asylum was built for the destitute, mentally ill, and poor of Providence, Rhode Island. In 1957 it was bought by Brown University, which demolished it the next year.

techniques were refined, yields grew, and surpluses could be stored or sold. Corn, cheese, and hay could all be sold or bartered, and a middle-class economy of relative abundance replaced subsistence.

Outside butchering services, weaving, and renting of draught animals or tools meant that individual families could manage farms and could grow. But the "all hands on deck" family model of farm management meant women and children did a large variety of tasks until industrialization made its mark and allowed education to become a necessity for every class of New England culture.

Nearly everyone based their lives around farms. Even ministers, doctors, and lawyers were usually employed part-time, with farming as their main occupation. Other professions such as tradesmen, crafts-men, and early industrialists, who used water power to make things, mainly based their livelihoods on serving farmers.

Wars are most cruel to civilians, and while the Revolutionary War meant a spike in business for those farmers who stayed down on the farm, after the victory the agriculture business faced hard times. Colo-nist farmers had farmed their small plots until the soil became worn out.

In the best of circumstances, New England had (and has) a terrible climate and even worse soil for farming. The best land, a precious few river valleys and coastal flatlands, were fairly well under production by the nineteenth century, so any new land made arable had limited upside.

Bad practices and worse natural conditions for providing suste-nance meant crop rotation, multiple pastures for one herd, fertilization, and new planting technologies had to be employed. For farms that did not improve and that could not provide for the family, sons and daugh-ters went off to towns and cities and sought work in factories, mills, and even on ships.

A Prize for Maine

The Burnham Tavern in Machias, Maine, was built about 1770. According to records in the Library of Congress, it was in the tavern where a band of volunteers made plans to fight back against a local Loyalist by capturing his merchant ships. In so doing, they also captured the accompanying British schooner HMS *Margaretta*, in the second naval battle of the Revolutionary War.

The Historic American Buildings Survey, the nation's first federal preservation program,

The tavern here is photographed from the rear in the 1930s by a photograph from the Historic American Building Survey. It has not changed at all in the many decades since the photo was taken.

thought enough of it to send a photographer there in 1937 to photograph the 1770 Burnham Tavern.

Although the 1937 account claims it as "the first sea battle of the Revolution," a claim also echoed by the still-standing tavern's website, that distinction was actually earned by the Battle of Fairhaven, which took place in Buzzards Bay, between New Bedford, Massachusetts, and Martha's Vineyard.

The chronicler, who may have been the photographer, continued: "After the battle the wounded soldiers from both sides were taken to the tavern for care. Here in this tavern, Captain Moore of the HMS *Margaretta*, who had been wounded in the battle, was taken. He died in one of the upper rooms."

The tavern's website says that "in recognition of its importance, the Burnham Tavern has been designated as a National Historic Site by the US Department of the Interior, and in 1974 the Tavern was selected as one of the 21 homes in the United States with the most significance to the American Revolution, the only one so selected in the State of Maine."

Today the tavern is open to the public from late June to early October.

Not Getting It the First Time, England Goes at It Again in 1812

Amid the first twenty years of forming a nation, America was getting into a fresh snit with its former Mother England. At least that part of the new country south of Long Island Sound was feeling that way.

New England's pragmatic and pro-business Federalist Party lost popularity as New England embraced the awakening Industrial Revolution and the creation of schools, an engine for innovation and culture creation. When the Democratic-Republican Party of Virginians Thomas Jefferson and James Madison led the charge to tame a frisky Britain from continued mischief with the new country's emancipation,

A BOXING MATCH, or Another Bloody Nose for JOHN BULL.

An early version of an editorial cartoon taunts the British over its naval losses during the War of 1812. It specifically hones in on the defeat of the HMS *Boxer* by an American ship in the fall of 1813. King George III, his face showing signs of a good beating, pleads, "Stop . . . Brother Jonathan, or I shall fall with the loss of blood . . . I must acknowledge your superior skill." James Madison, his opponent, says, "You thought yourself a 'Boxer,' did you?"

Fort Adams on Narragansett Bay

Because it was founded in war and seemed, to many, always to be in a state of war or preparation for war, the new United States needed good defenses.

In the nineteenth century one of the best defenses was a well-designed fortification.

Newport's Fort Adams was designed by Louis de Toussard, who served as an officer under Lafayette during the Revolution and who also designed West Point. Fort Adams was once the most complex fortification in the Western Hemisphere. Today's it is a state park and massive venue for events such as the Newport Jazz Festival and the Newport Folk Festival. But established on Independence Day in 1799 and named for President John Adams, Fort Adams became a first-line defense against all enemies.

The US Department of the Interior's application for the National Register says the "northeasterly thumblike protuberance" near the southwest end of Rhode Island "probably was first fortified in the late seventeenth century." The National Trust

A view looking north of the staircase at the fort.

The exterior of Fort Adams from the northwest.

Aerial View of Fort Adams, Newport, R. I.

An aerial view of Fort Adams in Newport, Rhode Island, taken in the mid-1950s.

nomination form notes that "William Brenton arrived in Newport in 1683 bearing a charter from King Charles I for an area now known as Brenton Point. He erected a house . . . and tradition holds that he ordered two cannon from England to protect his property from pirates and privateers." In 1740, fearing a French invasion, colonists built an observation post. Later, during the French and Indian War and even the Revolution, earthwork fortifications were built here.

In the nineteenth century, the new United States had the fort redesigned by Simon Bernard, former engineering aide to Napoleon, and by the first head of the US Army Corps of Engineers, Joseph Trotten. These two designed a fort able to mount 468 guns along a perimeter of more than 1,700 yards. It was built of Maine granite, shale, and brick, and could house 2,400 men. The fort was added onto, modified, and garrisoned until 1950.

Part of the fort is still used for housing by the US Navy.

In a view from the Potomac River, British forces under Major General Ross attack at Washington, D.C., in August 1814.

THE TAKING OF THE CITY OF WASHINGTON IN AMERICA

not a single Federalist voted to support the war—which we now know as the War of 1812.

This war is now mostly seen as an offshoot of the Napoleonic Wars between England and France, because both countries wanted to stop the other from trading with the resource-rich United States. England had additional reasons for embargoing American goods. Mostly it feared the United States had designs on its Canadian colonies and expansion to the west at a time when Great Britain was preoccupied with the French, but also because it was still reeling from the Revolutionary War.

In 1807, President Thomas Jefferson, who had had enough of war, got an embargo passed and imposed on American shipping so that the United States remained neutral in the war between England

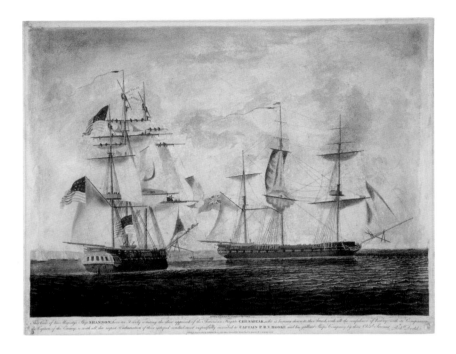

and France. This decision, however, affected New England most of all. Commerce with Britain in New England, it is estimated, fell by roughly 90 percent. Yet war came to the United States nevertheless.

Even when the British burned much of Washington, D.C., including the White House, New England was unmoved. The United States–imposed embargo against England caused a ruinous response because of an English blockade that virtually halted economic progress, especially in product-producing, trade-embracing, capital-seeking New England.

When negotiations ended the war in 1814, the British held onto a little part of Maine near the far north Canadian border. Maine, still the colonial possession of Massachusetts, felt resentment, which led to its own independence and statehood in 1820. That was part of the

Missouri Compromise, which New England ensured made Maine slavery-free and allowed Missouri to become a slave state.

Otherwise, the negotiated end of the war left New England largely untouched, except for a lower level of income. The loss of trade caused by the British embargo affected trade-happy New England more than any other part of America. The loss of export grew the New England spirit of self-reliance.

A Time of Inventiveness

New England's early embrace of technology allowed for more markets, better education in all things agricultural, and more efficient production both in agriculture and industry.

New technologies permitted a marked increase in production that served a rapidly growing population. Easing the early impact of new technologies was New England's natural resource of copious water power, which inevitably brought New England to the forefront of the looming Industrial Revolution, where it played a major role.

As its population grew, New Englanders needed greater agricultural production. Farms needed acreage to survive in the Little Ice Age's hostile growing season, but unfortunately most of New England's land that was not mountainous or sloped had suffered eons-old glacial carnage that had left typical New England farmlands rock filled and soil scraped.

To address the problem, deforestation proceeded at a rapid pace. Between the Revolution and the Civil War, less than half of New England's arable land was logged and made into farmland, more than doubling the agricultural dominance of the landscape and biosphere.

Elias Howe
Farm Boy, Inventor, Industrialist

Elias Howe was born in 1819 to a farming family who owned a gristmill in Spencer, Massachusetts. He had a progressive disability that hampered his ability to walk and to do the farm chores expected of all farm family members, but he did what he could. He left the farm to work at a textile mill in Lowell when he was sixteen.

Always interested in mechanical things, Howe worked in a mill until the financial panic of 1837 forced his move to Boston to find another job. There he found work making mariner's tools.

Machine shops in Boston were as high tech in 1837 as software companies in Silicon Valley are today. The energy of invention filled the city—and Howe's mind.

Portrait of Elias Howe, inventor of the sewing machine, from *Harper's Weekly*, 1867.

When Howe's progressive lameness forced him out of shop work in 1843, his wife took in sewing to support him and their three children. Howe saw the time it took to be a seamstress (14½ hours to sew together a shirt) and decided to give his full-time energy to create a sewing machine.

Howe found George Fisher, a local investor, who fronted him $500 for a half share in Howe's sewing machine idea. Two years later his ideas and determination made a machine that would sew—and Howe proved it in 1845 by sewing two suits, one for himself and the other for Fisher.

Howe got a US patent for his sewing machine in 1846. At first, nobody trusted his newfangled machine. Then, while Howe and Fisher were in England promoting their machine, his design was ripped off by multiple competitors. Howe spent the next five years in court getting his patent enforced, ultimately working out a deal with his competitors that gained him $2 million by the time of his death in 1867, coinciding with the expiration of his patent.

Thanks to his invention, a shirt could be sewn together in a fraction of the time.

The characteristics that made farming difficult helped make New England America's first industrial base. Its rocky hills and heavy snow meant rapidly flowing water that turned gravity into harnessable power. In the late eighteenth-century, England began to use machines to make textiles and iron tools using the strength of water power. After the Revolution those seeds spread to America: Founded in 1787, the Beverly (Massachusetts) Cotton Manufactury was the first cotton mill in America, followed rapidly by the Slater Mill and other factories in Pawtucket, Rhode Island; Maine; and soon all of New England.

Rock-Powered Water

Lemons, we now know, are essential to making lemonade.

The New England soils that broke unnumbered plows transformed America in an unanticipated way. Many thousands of years ago, glaciers crushed all of New England. Ice sheets were a mile thick and took 100,000 years to scour the entire landscape at a pace far slower than the slowest snail.

The most obvious result of this grinding advance to the Atlantic Ocean was Long Island, which was formed at the last leading edge of the glacial flow before it began its melting retreat when the last spate of global warming helped bring sea levels back up three hundred feet to their present levels.

In the ten thousand years since earth was freed from ice overload, millions of trees took root and grew to full forestation, blanketing New England in a verdant re-covering over ground once crushed beneath immeasurable layers of ice. Those forests must have made seventeenth-century colonists think they had landed upon a new Garden of Eden.

It's hard to fully imagine the depth of disappointment as trees felled to make arable farmland revealed countless rocks and acres of exposed bedrock. As roots of those felled trees were pulled up by teams of oxen, the mammoth depth and quantity of boulders was revealed. Prospects for productive farming must have made the Puritan's prayers similar to those hopeless pleas of Job's. How could a 70,000-square-mile rock garden produce enough corn and potatoes to feed those growing families?

Clearly, bedrock and soil that contains infinite bits and pieces of that bedrock, compressed over eons under gigatons of ice, would not allow seventeenth-century farming technology to be very productive. But initially, very few folks needed feeding. Also, forests were full of game, and the rivers, lakes, and sea were chock-full of protein.

But all those old scraped mountainsides, compressed moraines, and plowed landscapes meant that any amount of rainfall would not be absorbed below the surface very quickly. Lower permeability meant great flow of groundwater, and even old mountains are steep enough and glacier-scarred enough that the rivers and streams of New England were both everywhere and fast flowing.

Gravity made the glaciers crush, grind, and push every square inch of New England's topography, but gravity also made the same water that was tied up in those glacial floes flow with extreme velocity and power down the impermeable surfaces into steeply pitched streams and rivers. Energy can wreck, but harvested energy can be productive.

The sour landscape yielded a very sweet by-product: power. Before steam, before internal combustion, let alone before nuclear fission or fusion, New Englanders saw value in flowing water. In the eighteenth century, small factories sprang up where the water flowed fastest, using that power to turn wheels interlocked with spindles and

Before steam, before internal combustion, let alone before nuclear fission or fusion, New Englanders saw value in flowing water.

James Hillhouse
A New Haven Man

In 1761, when he was seven years old, James Hillhouse was sent from his home in Montville, Connecticut, to live with his childless aunt and uncle in New Haven.

The young Hillhouse ended up at Yale and seemed destined to follow his adoptive father's career path as a lawyer. But the Revolutionary War ended his legal career. During the war Hillhouse served as captain of Connecticut's Second Company of Governor's Foot Guard, the same position once held by Benedict Arnold.

After the war, Hillhouse became a civic promoter in extremis. He transformed downtown New Haven and its green by relentlessly planting elms and laying out the beginnings of the present-day Yale campus. He also took the lead in removing hundreds of remains from the graveyard behind Center Church and transferring them to Grove Street Cemetery, which he helped found in 1797 as the first privately held graveyard in the country. Hillhouse was also instrumental in the construction of the Farmington Canal.

Like many of the early New England multitaskers, Hillhouse ran for public office. He introduced an early antislavery bill into Congress, proposing that that Louisiana Purchase be made slave-free. He left the US Senate in 1810 to take charge of the Connecticut School Fund, building its coffers to the very large sum of $1.7 million over fifteen years. After Hillhouse's death, the city tapped that fund to build New Haven's first public high school in 1859, which is named for him.

It was land speculation, however, that enabled Hillhouse to leave a unique marker for the coming centuries. He bought a farm just outside downtown New Haven to create the finest "gated community" in the city—a two-block avenue on a wide street leading north from downtown. Over the next few generations, "the most beautiful street in America" (as observed by Charles Dickens and possibly Mark Twain) was built, and today the dozens of nineteenth-century villas set back from a double row of majestic trees remain largely preserved—including the Yale president's mansion.

Not surprisingly, it's named Hillhouse Avenue.

Hillhouse Avenue No. 47, view along Hillhouse Avenue toward Sachem's Wood.

Hillhouse Avenue No. 65, view along Hillhouse Avenue toward Sachem's Wood.

wheels into gristmills that processed grain and sawmills that cut lumber. Fifty years before the Industrial Revolution changed everything, water power made living in the terrible farmland of New England a little easier.

Samuel Slater had started out as an apprentice for the owner of a cotton mill in Derbyshire, England. Eventually rising to the position of superintendent, he became intimately familiar with the brilliantly effective water-powered mill machines designed by Richard Arkwright. Slater memorized the workings of the machinery and quietly found his way to Pawtucket, Rhode Island, in 1789.

Why Pawtucket of all places and not raucous Boston or prosperous Tory-friendly New York? Because the Blackstone River, which runs from Worcester, Massachusetts, to Providence drops 438 feet over forty-six miles, and travels through Pawtucket, picking up head every inch of the way. Slater partnered with local Quaker Moses Brown. The combination of English technology, Quaker work ethic, and the power of gravity created the Slater Mill, which not only transformed textile production forever but ultimately filled the banks of the Blackstone River with factories.

Industrialist Samuel Slater.

Slater, like so many New Englanders, even those newly transplanted, ran upstream with his success, building many more factories and the first entire mill-based town, Slatersville, Rhode Island, in 1803, finally settling (and building more mills) in Webster, Massachusetts.

The success spawned many applications. Eli Terry built a water-powered clock factory in Connecticut in 1802, and Francis Lowell harnessed the Charles River to create the first mechanized cotton gin in 1812; by 1813 there was another in Newport, New Hampshire. Later the Monadnock Mills in Claremont, New Hampshire, became the largest textile mills on the upper Connecticut River by 1830.

This photo of the Yale-Duryea Mills in Stockbridge, Berkshire County, Massachusetts, shows the lower mill, water wheel, cistern, and race (or flume). The mill opened in 1823.

Cheap power meant technology was invented to use it. Jobs followed, farms failed or collapsed into bigger farms, and whole families moved to towns that became cities. Tenements replaced houses, and factories replaced home craftsmanship. An entire culture pivoted from subsistence farming and local artisans to production farms, factories, and railroads and canals, with New England, as usual, leading the way in America.

Samuel Morse
From Painting to Communications

Born in 1791, Samuel Morse is a unique figure in the cultural revolutions that sparked in nineteenth-century New England. The Morse family also valued education and sent Samuel to Phillips Academy in Andover, Massachusetts, at age seven.

Unfortunately for the family's Calvinist work ethic, Morse's aptitude trended to the fine arts. His painting studies at Yale were his best subjects, but his parents insisted on a practical career and sent him into publishing and book-keeping at a bookstore in his hometown of Charlestown, Massachusetts.

After a miserable year, his parents relented and provided for Morse to go to England to study art at the Royal Academy. He was in England at the time of the War of 1812, and the experience made him a devotedly patriotic American. Returning to create a studio in Boston, Morse started his career in painting. Portraiture became Morse's way of turning his artistic expression into a money-making career—no doubt making his father a happy man. His friendly persona gained him many famous commissions, including with the Marquis de Lafayette, James Fenimore Cooper, Eli Whitney, Noah Webster, and two presidents.

But art was only one side of Samuel F. B. Morse's professional life. He was always creating "gadgets," sometimes with his brother Sidney.

Samuel Morse in a photo by Matthew Brady between 1855 and 1865.

Failed attempts at a water pump for fire engines and a marble-cutting machine did not dissuade Morse from thinking about technology amid his artistic endeavors. During this time, he met and married Susan Walker Morse in Concord, New Hampshire. Three children followed, and in many ways the young Morse family had a lovely life.

In February 1825, Morse's wife Susan became very ill while Morse was in Washington. The message that she was in dire health reached Morse days after Susan became sick, and it took Morse days to return to New Haven to find his wife already buried. Morse was devastated by her death. Morse focused his energy on finding a way to use the new technologies of the young Industrial Revolution to make instantaneous communication possible.

A journey to Europe for his art career brought Morse into contact with Charles Thomas Jackson. Jackson was a scientist deeply engaged in the new field of electromagnetism. The two men began to work on a new way to use a single-wire method of communicating with electricity.

Others in France and Germany were already working along similar lines but used multiple wires and created impractical ways to transmit electric signals. But Morse and Jackson finally evolved an American version in 1837.

But Morse's actual transmission language, Morse code, may just be Samuel Morse's one

A stereographic photo of the Samuel Morse statue in New York's Central Park.

Samuel Morse lived in a "villa"—a home built with lumber that combined Tuscan tower and cornice elements with the carefully carpentered precision of New England craftsmanship.

abiding and unique personal contribution to a technology that was sweeping the world. Just as Steve Jobs invented very little save the means of using existing technologies, the genius of Morse was in creating a useful, efficient tool where others often failed.

Morse's relentless pursuit of recognition ultimately resulted in his version of the technology becoming the worldwide standard that was employed for the next one hundred years. Endless honors followed, and he achieved a level of acclaim that his artwork had failed to do.

While running water facilitated industrialization, it was water heated above 212 degrees Fahrenheit that pushed power beyond the flowing water or its source. You only needed a place to build a very hot fire, which meant coal became valuable, which meant more railroads, which meant more iron, more foundries, more specialists, and on and on.

In 1800, one in fifty free adults had a clock. But who needed a clock to know when to plow, plant, and eat? Within a generation, however, the factories that made clocks (mostly in Connecticut), as well as all the other products in all the other factories in New England, created an economy that defined a workday by hours, not seasons. Economic opportunity creates both the means to better supply the demands of consumers and ever-increasing demands for new products that in turn transform lives, communities, countries, and cultures.

Water flows downhill, but humanity, especially in New England, relentlessly aspires to the bigger, the better, the greater. It's why lemonade tastes better than water.

Milling Southern Cotton in New England

All that water gushing throughout New England's bony hills and valleys powered the machinery of the Industrial Revolution. It helped build furniture, clocks, machines of various types, and luxury goods.

But nothing else that water could do equaled the employment and profit of textile mills.

The Slater Mill in Pawtucket, Rhode Island, was the first water-powered spinning mill to use the British Arkwright system of

Left: A view from the southwest elevation of the Slater Mill, Pawtucket, Rhode Island.

Top, right: The southwest turbine on the ground floor of the Slater Mill in Pawtucket, RI.

carding and spinning in North America and the country's first successful cotton factory.

The two-and-one-half-story wood-frame building, with pitched roof and trapdoor monitor, was restored in the 1920s to its 1835 appearance. The earliest part of the mill was constructed by Samuel Slater in 1793. This included spinning machines, water sluice, and dam.

The mill was added onto in the early 1800s, and bit by bit, a bell tower and a spinning mule (probably the country's first piece of the relative complex but essential looming machinery) were added, then other additions came in the mid- to late nineteenth century.

Newer mills were built after the Civil War in Southern states, where people worked for less money and rushing water was plentiful. These mills were also closer to the cotton fields, so transportation was less of an issue. This, along with more Northern mill competition, eventually took business away from Slater. In 1955, the mill complex became a museum that now exhibits original operational textile machines.

The mill was added to the National Register of Historic Places and designated a National Historic Landmark in 1966, and in 2014 the mill became part of the new Blackstone River Valley National Historical Park in Lincoln, Rhode Island.

An aerial view of the Slater Mill and the Blackstone River running through Pawtucket, Rhode Island.

Water in another form led to larger factories nowhere near rapidly flowing water and, in turn (and perhaps just as significantly), created train transportation that compressed the markets. New York grain could make New England bread. New England shoes could be put on New York feet. Ultimately, steam-powered trains ran westward to better land and growing seasons, which meant grain became bounteous and cheap. As cities grew to respond to the new opportunities of factory technology, New England farmers transitioned to creating perishable food meant for local consumption that, unlike grain, could not be shipped—such as milk, meat, and vegetables, for city folk who had one of the new office or industrial jobs.

Beyond making better goods more cheaply and creating huge profits for early industrialists, the mills' sweeping change transformed all of New England in the first half of the nineteenth century. Between 1830 and 1860, thousands of farm girls left their rural homes in New England to work in the mills.

As the textile industry grew, the production of leather goods, copper, and paper also led to an astonishing increase in factory building and manufacture, which required immigration that supplanted farm-girl recruitment. While New England's robust and unsentimental antislavery movement prohibited immigration from Africa in 1808, the pre–Civil War immigrants came primarily from Ireland, a wave of immigration that accelerated during the Irish potato famine of 1846.

Even though they needed the labor, the reaction in Boston, the major receiving port, was not good. Old Puritanical Yankee fears of a papist invasion spawned the Know-Nothing Party, which was dead set against the open immigration policy that brought many of the Irish to America in the first place.

As more and more Midwestern farms sent their cheaper agricultural goods to New England, New England farmers recognized a need to reform their practices or go out of business. New agricultural societies sprang up, abetted by an increased focus on education in New England to grow and spread invention of new products, methods, and insights.

Miles and Miles of More Mills

At its peak, the Amoskeag Mill, running more than a mile along each side of New Hampshire's Merrimack River, was the world's largest textile mill.

The huge Amoskeag Mill was built between 1838 and 1915.

Built and enlarged between 1838 and 1915, with the largest concentration of mill buildings on the river's east shore, the original name was the Amoskeag Manufacturing Company. Within its vast land area along the river, the company created something of a manufacturing mall by selling chunks of land and what it called mill privileges to these other companies.

Companies included the Stark Corporation, Manchester Mills, Amoskeag New Mills (separate from the manufacturing company), and the Manchester Locomotive Works built in 1854.

When it shuttered operations in 1935, a large group of Manchester, New Hampshire, citizens bought the complex and renamed it Amoskeag Industries, whose business was selling parcels of the giant complex to other companies and manufacturers.

Facing page: Workers leaving the Amoskeag Mill in Manchester, New Hampshire, 1909.

At its height, the Amoskeag Mill was the largest cotton textile facility in the world.

Encompassing 15,000 acres, the mill employed up to seventeen thousand workers.

"Amoskeag Industries is a for-profit company owned by more than one hundred stock holders whose primary purpose is to promote economic development for Manchester," the company's website says. "The board of directors, currently made up of fourteen community leaders, meets quarterly to review economic conditions, consider actions that will encourage economic growth, and seek out economic opportunities that will enhance the greater Manchester area quality of life and instill civic pride."

Since its 1936 incorporation, "fifty-four businesses were established in the mill yard such as Pacific Mills, Chicopee Mills, Amoskeag Worsted Mills, and Waumbec Mills." Further, "Amoskeag has participated in a number of significant projects and transactions over the years including Victory Park, the Brown Avenue Industrial Park, Pine Island

Park, the establishment of the UNH Manchester facility, the sale of the Ash Street School, the city's original high school, and the Hillsborough County Courthouse," according to the North Project Amoskeag Industries' website.

Moving New England's Goods Across the Continent

The country was moving westward, and the market was exploding. Millions of new urban dwellers would need food and houses, and the once-novel railroad could get it to them. As the new infrastructure allowed for effective and affordable shipping, farmers could use the better and cheaper tools produced by new industrial technologies—like cast-iron plows, mowing machines, and horse-rakes—for increased and more efficient production.

Beyond creating new means of transportation, the tools and techniques that industrialized New England allowed—even required—that new agricultural products be produced. Tobacco, potash, charcoal, and fuel wood were among those either helped along by the new technologies or required by those technologies to power their revolutionary impact.

New markets and products were accompanied by the inevitable benefits of industrialization, making other necessities much cheaper, transforming a local craftsman ethic into a machine-based mass-produced and mass-distributed sourcing of products—cloth, housewares, and tools soon were bought not made, saving both time and money, and transforming an artisanal economy to the split system of rural agriculture and urban product production.

Covered Bridges: A New England Innovation to Cross Those Money-Making Streams

Wood-covered bridges were neither invented in nor exclusive to New England. The world's first covered bridge was likely built in China about two thousand years ago. They exist in many other states and have been built all over the world. But since the covered-bridge boom ended, fewer than half of the eight hundred survivors (from a high of an estimated twelve thousand) still span rivers in this country.

It's hard to say what makes the covered bridge a New England icon; perhaps it's the heroically picturesque and shady repose of these sheds over surging water that's so evocative of the rolling landscape of inland New England.

The simple "king post" bridges constructed before the nineteenth century needed huge timbers and very careful construction to withstand the loads imposed even over relatively short spans.

But two Connecticut designers, architect Ithiel Town of New Haven and Theodore Burr of Torrington, created their own systems, which were replicated all across America (Town's design made him wealthy). Later, laminated arches and other innovations extended the usefulness of wood truss bridges into the twentieth century. Ultimately, iron, then steel and concrete, overwhelmed any viability the romantic covered bridge had for transportation infrastructure.

As with most things that have been romanticized, the origins of New England's covered bridges were purely practical.

First, as subsistence farming gave way to production farming and factory goods supplanted homemade goods, there was great and

Cornish-Windsor
covered bridge.

Built in 1872, the Sunday River Bridge (also called the Artist's Covered Bridge) in Newry, Maine, holds the honor of being the most photographed and painted covered bridge in the state.

growing need for transportation. Factory products had to be shipped, and this meant more and better roads, and then trains.

Second, New England had the flowing rivers that begat the first wave of water-powered industrialization. But those fast-flowing rivers meant fording or short-span bridges simply would not work.

Third, wood was everywhere, and millwrights made everything, so local technologies in rural settings were more practical than importing iron from distant factories. This meant trusses versus beams or cables.

Fourth, weather impacts transportation, so ice and snow on bridges that are much colder and freeze over sooner than dirt roads meant keeping snow and ice off a bridge in the first place was easier than plowing or shoveling. So, voilà! The sides of the trusses were walled, and the trusses supported roofs that shed both ice and snow.

So the methods and means of barn building fused with engineering precision and down-home aesthetics to make an aesthetic singularity. The unique presence of an extruded agrarian barn form that spans a stream from stone pier to stone pier, covered top and sides with vernacular architectural detailing straight from local farmhouses, or later from an nineteenth-century architectural pattern book, is somehow completely compelling and often lovely to behold.

Muscular engineering used in graceful ways with hands-on craftsmanship results in a charming sort of oxymoronic aesthetic combination. That charm has sparked many devotional societies for covered-bridge preservation, especially in New England, where inland development has slowed to a snail's pace, removing economic capacity and incentive for replacement by dumber, lower maintenance products of twentieth-century engineering.

From Factory Towns through Two World Wars

5

Without catastrophic changes caused by external events (like the Revolutionary War), cultures tend to reinforce rather than forget the values they embody. The once-plowed field of the eighteenth century's Great Awakening found new voice in industrializing, formerly slavery-tolerating early nineteenth century New England. As people advocated for a God-centric life, it became intellectually and morally impossible to accept that the image of God is present in every person except that one race of the enslaved. Slavery, so essential to one half of the country, became completely intolerable to New England's culture.

Abolitionists like William Lloyd Garrison and Wendell Phillips were New Englanders, and the region was home to antislavery politicians like John Quincy Adams, Charles Sumner, and John P. Hale. Rhode Island was the first state to emancipate all slaves within its borders in 1784. The Republican Party was formed as an abolitionist party in the 1850s, with all of New England its geographic base.

Facing page: New England was well represented in the Abolition movement by a relentless collection of anti-slavery activists. Clockwise from top left: John Quincy Adams, Wendell Phillips, William Lloyd Garrison, and John P. Hale.

As America matured in the first 80 years of its existence, New England leapt into the beginnings of an economic and cultural dynamic that is still shaping us today. Education, technology, and infrastructure are at the core of every discussion of a twenty-first-century future. New England grabbed those abiding engines of innovation 200 years ago, just like it embraced personal freedom 156 years before the rest of the country decided to fight for those values.

When Eli Whitney left Massachusetts to work at a Georgia plantation in 1792, seven hundred thousand slaves toiled the fields. He invented the cotton gin in 1794. By the time the Civil War broke out in 1860, about three million slaves worked for Southern masters on vast cotton plantations, planting, weeding, picking, and feeding cotton into Whitney's voracious gin, sometimes powered by water, but often by a horse or even slaves.

Thanks to Whitney, Yankee ingenuity put the genteel Southern agrarian economy on steroids. The economic clout of the South was based not only on the cotton gin but also on its three million unpaid laborers, who took care of every task at a very small price tag, if you disregard the moral bankruptcy of slavery.

Cotton production expanded from 750,000 bales in 1830 to 2.85 million bales in 1850, in great part due to Whitney.

Cotton production expanded from 750,000 bales in 1830 to 2.85 million bales in 1850, in great part due to Whitney. The gin allowed cotton to be processed and shipped out to the mills of New England faster. It also meant that the ability to process cotton outpaced planting and growth of cotton, which then had to be stepped up. Once those many more thousands of acres were planted, more field hands were needed to pick it and haul it. And that required more slaves.

Although against slavery, New England was ready to arm the South with all the gins it needed. New England, the country's tiny but mighty manufacturing center, also was busy cranking out firearms, the tools that eventually would put an end to slavery.

The New England Contribution

New England, especially its most educated and cultured class in Boston and the surrounding area, was perhaps even more attuned to the outrage of slavery than the rest of its northern neighbors, as the South's use of humans as machines flew in the face of its Puritan-rooted culture.

Leading up to the reckoning of the Civil War, the War of 1812 proved just how profitable arming a country with a fully mechanized industrial base can be. By 1860, Boston, Springfield, New Haven, and Hartford boomed by creating the tools of war, while in virtually every other town something was being manufactured for the war. Eli Whitney, Samuel Colt, and Oliver Winchester made Connecticut the "Armory of America."

The Civil War was the most heinous and divisive of the three wars that shaped America. Every other region of the country had experienced some direct damage to its infrastructure in these conflicts, but New England kept building the factories, railroads, and the support systems necessary to create the weaponry that laid waste to so much of the twenty-plus states that saw action on the ground during the Civil War.

By 1860 New England had made firearms for years, but the Civil War jump-started its armament production. Because of moral outrage, including confidence in its ability to win, New England was not shy in its support of the Union in the Civil War. Sixty percent of

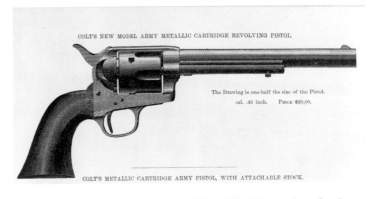

COLT'S NEW MODEL ARMY METALLIC CARTRIDGE REVOLVING PISTOL.

The Drawing is one-half the size of the Pistol.
cal. .45 inch.   Price $20,00.

COLT'S METALLIC CARTRIDGE ARMY PISTOL, WITH ATTACHABLE STOCK.

The 1879 Colt revolver fired a .45 caliber bullet and came with a hefty price tag of $20.

Massachusetts men (only men could vote) voted for Midwesterner Abraham Lincoln, which reflected the widespread feelings the anti-slavery movement had formed with great conviction since the 1830s. The fervor, which was abetted by the religious resurgence of the Great Awakening, was welcomed not only by industrialists seeing a profit center but in the churches of their great-great-grandfathers and the colleges where their children were enrolled.

The six-state Armory of New England gave almost 360,000 of its sons to the war and lost 40,000 of them in the effort. As with the rest of the country, army units were formed geographically, so entire towns could have their young male demographic devastated in one costly battle. Drive through any New England city or town and somewhere in each is a monument to the war dead erected during the decades after the war.

The band of the First Connecticut Heavy Artillery strike a pose on the James River in Virginia, April 1865.

Making a Name for Themselves in the Fight Against Slavery

New England's culture of industry, hard work, and success accounting for more than class or lineage, was perhaps what most clearly distinguished the region from the genteel South, where manners, "good families," and the land were central to its way of life.

New England's burgeoning industrialism and fervor for technology and education was at the leading edge of a changing America. It could be said that New England had the first encounter with town-to-city density in one generation, as immigrants flooded a demographic where

Officers of Third Regiment,
Massachusetts Heavy
Artillery pose at Fort Totten in
Washington, D.C., during the
closing months of the Civil War.

more than 10 percent of men who went to fight (at prime working age) died in the Civil War.

With the full impact of the steam engine taking an existing waterpower-fed industrial base to the cutting edge of technological sophistication and efficiency by 1860, the Civil War exploded the impact and scope of New England's infrastructure to spur on a century's dominance in many industries.

When the war ended, production diversified, encouraged by the fully formed rail infrastructure linking New England internally and to every other part of America. The safe harbor of Boston was the epicenter of sea-going trade for New England, but an expanding rail system could easily receive goods from every producer in the region. The production of clocks, hats, textiles, ships, brass, and firearms were woven into the hearts of New England cities.

New England, the American tech center of the nineteenth century, largely supplanted the heaven-focused mission of its first settlers. Although far more religious then than present-day New England, by the Civil War the theocracies of Plymouth and New Haven were completely gone. Universities like Yale, Harvard, and Dartmouth, while branded with their religious origins, became secular intellectual powerhouses in the first half of the twentieth century.

The twinned ascendance of education and infrastructure spurred the density that began to fuse scores of New England coastal towns into one homogenized settled landscape, punctuated by denser places like Boston, Providence, New Haven, and Bridgeport, while increasingly farming became an inland use of land.

Manufacturing overtook agriculture as the financial basis of the New England economy after the Civil War. Here were jobs for anyone willing to work, because land ownership was not a prerequisite for survival. Immigrants flowed into ports as goods sailed out until the Civil War. New England was really Little England in its provenance, but industrialization made unskilled labor a draw for the new residents, and New England's population grew by 150 percent.

This new diversification of the population was needed in service of the machinery of technology. Meanwhile the offspring of the colonists dominated the academic realms and the ownership of industry. Neighborhoods became outposts of "the old country" of newcomers, often becoming distinct enclaves that combined the worker class with cultural distinctions. It was in that way that Boston became the home of the "fighting Irish" before South Bend.

In the twentieth century, electric power plants drew coal from other parts of the country as railroads became lifelines not only for factories but for a new century that saw radios become the hearth of

A 1916 bird's-eye view of
Hartford, Connecticut, after a
snowfall.

the home and lighting become non–flame based. In New England, oil
and gas had to be imported, so railroads and highways helped integrate
a region that needed fossil fuels but had few of them. The next era
created a highway system that rewrote the architectural legacy of many
neighborhoods, but the roads and rails of the first half of the twentieth
century also cut paths through cities to reach factories, power plants,
and ports.

More than any other region of the United States, New England saw a full-on transition of the landscape once devoted to town autonomy become a place of common infrastructure. Greens became parks, meetinghouses were abandoned for new town halls, and businesses were less "family" and more "work."

The natural independent spirit of farmers and niche industrialists at the mid-nineteenth century served to carry on the spirit of the original colonial mind-set: hard work within the biblical framework of God's will. God may have become literally less part of every law and social system but, as the decades rolled on into the twentieth century, the reality of tradition, the work of many earlier generations and their values and aesthetics, immersed New England life in a place that could see a bright future but still remember the past.

All through New England, the colonial perfection of the green, meetinghouse, covered bridge, and period main streets with historic houses bearing dates and names, combined with Currier and Ives's brand of nostalgia and romance to make "colonial" architecture the default for the preponderance of residential building by the time of World War II.

For New England the time between the Civil War and World War II saw a small part of American farmland go fallow, while multistory iron, steel, brick, and timber buildings flooded many of its towns and cities with shops and factories that replaced jobs in farming.

Giant, elegantly spare and clean buildings with open interiors filled with natural light from huge windows and skylights became the working-class meetinghouses and replaced the barns of the countryside. Jobs meant a huge influx of immigrants and an infusion of new cultures that ended New England's white, English, and Protestant homogeneity forever.

Still Fishing: The First New England Industry

Two hundred years before the Pilgrims, the Puritans, and everybody else who decided to live in New England, explorers noted an overwhelming abundance of fish here.

Similar to the Midwest's buffalo population in the nineteenth century, an absence of natural predators in the Atlantic made cod and

This image of Bar Harbor, Maine, shows a winding network of weirs. The photo was taken sometime between 1900 and 1915.

other "groundfish" (those living near the bottom of relatively shallow banks) so abundant that, in 1602, English explorer Bartholomew Gosnold changed the name of Cape Saint James to Cape Cod.

Two factors made New England fishing the foremost industry (and arguable the only profitable one) over the course of four hundred years of development in the region.

First the coastline has a complicated edge, a shoreline that created not only harbors but habitats. Also, that coast is long—about 6,000 miles long if you could unfold it. Maine alone has almost 3,500 miles (without all its undulations that would be about 230 miles, including the only North American fjord).

Second, the huge underwater banks that start in New England stretch up to Newfoundland and create perfect habitats for many species of fish. The depth of the water and the currents create the perfect temperature for cod and other groundfish to spawn and thrive.

Aboard a trap fishing boat, the end of the trip, Provincetown, Massachusetts, 1937–1940.

Throughout its history New England fed itself, and then the world, with this abundance. Thousands of small boats harvested not only fish but also shellfish and bivalves. Subsistence fishing became commercialized, and unlike the paucity of viable New England farmland and warm weather, the nineteenth century saw the market respond to abundance. By 1880 more than four hundred fishing vessels sailed out of Gloucester, Massachusetts, alone. While factories absorbed the Irish in Boston and Connecticut, the Portuguese came in droves to fish in Gloucester in the twentieth century.

Rudyard Kipling wrote *Captains Courageous* in 1897, describing the lives of "salt bankers" as they fished out of Gloucester. The ethic was virtually the same as recounted by Sebastian Junger's modern bestseller *The Perfect Storm* in 1997, set in the same locale.

Theresa and Dan **fishing vessel out of Gloucester, 1942.**

Fishermen at work,
Provincetown, 1937–1940.

Fishing was and is a dangerous business. So many died making
a living at it that in the nineteenth-century, schooner designs were
changed to provide safer sailing for fishermen. But in the end the
industrialization of the ships and procedures changed everything.
Steam-powered trawlers from England ramped up harvests to extreme
levels in the early twentieth century. In 1930, thirty-seven million haddock were caught, but ninety million baby haddock were killed, which
wrecked future harvests.

Overfishing dampened profits, but so did the food preferences.
Children of the first wave of mass immigration in the late nineteenth
and early twentieth centuries came to think of fish as less desirable than
meat. But World War II made any and all protein a necessary provision
for its war effort.

While lobsters and clamming operations remain small by comparison, the 1960s saw an international explosion of competitors, as huge
floating fish factories from the Soviet Union, Japan, Poland, Spain, and
East Germany further overfished New England's ocean banks.

Regulations tried to limit the damage and protect America's stake in the industry, but the environmental cost is still in free fall, with overfishing yet to stop and the cascade-like failure of entire species of haddock, hake and herring, as well as cod.

Religion, agriculture, and manufacturing have ebbed in twenty-first century New England, but from the very first moment ashore, New Englanders fished. If good planning and common sense prevail, it will be part of New England for its next four hundred years.

A Revolution of Work Itself

From nation-stirring literature to the creation of technologies that sent man to the moon, New England's scribblers, thinkers, tinkerers, scientists, and oddballs sprang to exultant activity in the time between the last of our wars with England and World War I. It's difficult to pinpoint another period in American history when inventiveness flowered to its highest potential, as it did in New England during the time surrounding the nineteenth century, though it makes sense in a country that invented itself.

The first patent issued under the 1790 Patent Act, was to Vermonter Samuel Hopkins for his process for making potash, a key fertilizer constituent. No laws or regulations were needed to spur the mechanically minded, motivated, well-educated, and geographically gifted citizens of New England.

The invasion of huge factories—and along with them, tenements, pollution, and the gigantic amounts of money being made by the new industrialist elite—transformed formerly wee towns. They became places of huge production facilities, as fossil fuels fed them and all the contributing infrastructure was geared to move raw material in and finished goods out.

The extreme profits leveraged by hard work and entrepreneurship created a donor subeconomy, where patrons built libraries, museums, and academic enclaves. Amid these large-order constructions (that often exploded without planning or thoughtful design), the infill of housing for workers meant humans lived cheek by jowl on the leftover land.

As industry grew, fed by America's growing military dominance, farming technology helped feed more people using fewer acres, even with a single growing season and fields sewn amid rocks and hillsides.

The Billings Farm and Museum in Woodstock, Vermont, is a working farm dedicated to educating others on the scientific-farming history through interactive exhibits and demonstrations.

The result was fewer farms, but those remaining were bigger. The westward advance of agribusiness to areas that had flat fields with thirty inches of topsoil bathed in eight months of productive farming weather meant less in New England food was grown on its own land.

Because cities grew to the point where no food was produced within miles, a culture of commerce arose to feed off the amazing increase in productivity that industrialization made necessary. Trails became roads that became paved two-way streets, with trucks, traffic lights, and development to sustain those on their way. Just as water power became inefficient and abandoned, horses were replaced with automobiles.

Not limited to New England, of course, this transition from subsistence to a scattered economy in which people did not live where they worked, or often even near it, created the beginnings of a modern economy in the twentieth century. People no longer bartered for goods but were paid in cash for working for someone else. This escalated to the point where "workers" became a class, as did "middle."

Skipping School
When We Put Our Children to Work

Full employment for adults in New England's many factories and mills left little slack in the labor pool. So, with no laws to prevent it, industry owners turned to the children of the poor.

At the turn of the twentieth century, it was common to employ children as young as six to work, often in dangerous conditions, in mills, canneries, factories, and as messengers.

These children, including many immigrants who spoke little or no English, were the young sweepers, "doffers," spinners, carders, pickers,

stackers, runners, and newsboys in the new century's first couple of decades. Some were illiterate, some malnourished, a few injured or disfigured by accidents on the job.

All of these children were exploited as cheap labor, a practice that occurred all over the United States but was pervasive in the many mills and supporting industries that operated in the South and especially in New England. Although widespread, child labor was not something that mill owners and operators and other manufacturing industries wanted to have publicized.

The notion of young children working in often dangerous industrial conditions was becoming contentious because most adults in the country thought such child labor was wrong. The National Child Labor Committee (NCLC) was formed in 1904 to promote "the rights, awareness, dignity, well-being and education of children and youth as they relate to work and working." About one out

Left: The photographer Lewis Hine took this and other photos of working children for the National Child Labor Committee. This is a photo of Addie Card, described in Hine's notes as an "anemic little spinner in North Pownal Cotton Mill" in Vermont.

of six young children (five to ten years old) held "gainful occupations."

To increase awareness, the NCLC hired Lewis Hine, a professional photographer, to go into the mines, factories, fields, streets, and any other places where children were put to work, and document their labor and working conditions. Reaction was strong; states worked together, and in 1912 the federal government created the United States Children's Bureau, an agency formed to improve the lives of children and families, which today is under the Department of Health and Human Services.

Above: Hine captioned this January 1912 photo as "Young doffer and spinner boys in Seaconnet Mill. The youngest are Manuel Perry, 111 Pitman St., John E. Mello, 229 Alden St., Manuel Louis. None of these could write their own names. The last couldn't spell the street he lives on. They spoke almost no English."

Below: Boys in a New England factory.

This photograph was taken in an Easthampton, Massachusetts, mill. Hine described it as "two young spinners at the close of a week's work leaving the cotton mill in Easthampton, Mass."

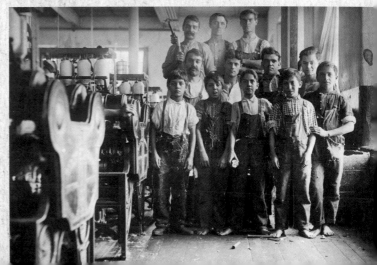

Memorial Hall with statue
of John Harvard, at Harvard
College (1890).

The Sheffield-Sterling-Strathcona
Hall at Yale University.

Building a
New Culture

6

Until a revolution leveled the playing field for white males, and a Civil War unified the country into New England's model of a free market economy where people with brains and ingenuity could express themselves, the full potential of meritocracy and middle class could not happen. Underclasses abounded in the waves of European immigrants, freed slaves, and their offspring that flooded into New England. And the intellectual watershed of New England's academic infrastructure that was second to none in America, and soon the world, meant that brawn had less traction for success than brains in a society turning its back on agriculture.

As scions of industry sought to legitimize their wealth culturally, New England saw the largesse of old-time trickle-down philanthropy on a scale that rivaled the royals' entitled noblesse oblige. Following the lead of John D. and Abby Rockefeller in Colonial Williamsburg, an investment banker bought the town of Grafton, Vermont, to preserve it. Harvard and Yale hired the same architect, James Gamble Rogers, to create American versions of England's Oxford and Cambridge in New England.

In the first half of the twentieth century the desire for intellectual credibility in the eyes of the world became very important to a region that had completely bootstrapped itself into wealth. Cultural institutions received the excess income from many second- and third-generation descendants of nineteenth-century wealth. Those donated profits helped to create a full-on academic class centered largely in New England, where five out of seven Ivies and MIT became part of academic "branding" before the word was invented.

Just as tenements and trade schools provided the machines of the industrial world with manpower enough for profitable production, private prep schools, also built on the British model (i.e., public schools like Eton) became the feeder system for a robust collegiate hothouse. St. Paul's, St. Mark's, Exeter, and Groton became the prototypes for a legitimate precollegiate education for the right young men.

Great sports venues and arts havens, from Fenway Park, to the Hartford Athenaeum, to Boston Symphony Hall, popped up as repositories of both excess wealth and to support the new idea of "recreation," where even twelve-hour days had time off and Sunday was still the Sabbath. Huge cathedrals were built for largely Catholic immigrants to thank God for that day off, though a Sunday afternoon ball game or concert could provide a small antidote to the drudgery.

Like the Adirondacks, the Berkshires, Martha's Vineyard, coastal Rhode Island, and coastal Maine, Connecticut's Litchfield County soon became the hot-weather retreat of the in-city elites.

World Series, Fenway Park, American League Grounds, October 12, 1914. Boston Braves defeated the Philadelphia Athletics, 5–4 in 12 innings. The Braves had been in last place in July and went on to win the National League pennant by 10½ games. They borrowed Fenway from the Red Sox for the season, because their home field was old and run down.

Uniquely New England

P. T. Barnum: "Prince of Humbug"

At age fifteen, Phineas Taylor Barnum's father, Philo, died, and Phineas became responsible for supporting his widowed mother and his four younger siblings.

P. T. liquidated the family farm and opened a store, but (like his grandfather) he started a career dedicated to making mirth via shock.

Barnum used "headwork" in his early years to create a lottery, a newspaper, and ultimately "The Greatest Show on Earth." His big break came in 1835 when he happened upon a black woman named Joice Heth who was being marketed as 160 years old. A year of touring the very ancient-appearing Heth proved to Barnum that oddities, fake or real, generated huge interest—and money.

Barnum used Heth's death in 1836 to generate even more interest, by selling tickets to her autopsy and celebrating the revealed fraud that she was but half her claimed age. Barnum spent his life making money from every possible attention-getter, including his own self-celebrated release from prison after he served time for defaming a local deacon in his paper, the *Herald of Freedom*.

He built a mermaid—"Feejee"—from a monkey head and torso stitched to a fish's tail. He bought a huge elephant, Jumbo, and made more money and fame using it to display the Brooklyn Bridge's structural soundness. Barnum discovered a tiny four-year-old who stayed tiny and put him on tour for decades as Tom Thumb—so successfully that he and Charles Stratton (Thumb's real name) became partners. He found high-brow hucksterism in promoting a Swedish opera singer,

Phineas T. Barnum around 1860, when he would have been about fifty years old, during a financially troubled time for him and before he was elected to public office, first as a state representative from Fairfield, Connecticut, and later as mayor of Bridgeport.

Iranistan, P.T. Barnum's Moorish Revival mansion in Bridgeport, Connecticut, of which he said, "The whole was built and established literally 'regardless of expense,' for I had no desire even to ascertain the entire cost."

Jenny Lind, as the greatest voice ever heard, even though he had never heard her.

He created museums in New York and Bridgeport that suffered many fires, went bankrupt, and rebounded using speaking fees and writing on the theme of *The Art of Money Getting*. His autobiography capitalized on revealing his frauds by selling over one million copies in his lifetime. Barnum ultimately sold more than eighty-two million

The Greatest Show on Earth poster shows Barnum with one of his exhibits, including the skeleton of Jumbo the elephant, "The colossal and prodigious frame of the largest and noblest animal that ever lived. The only elephant skeleton ever publicly exhibited." It goes on to promise "a strange & amazing show without a parellel [*sic*]. Mounted by Prof. Henry A. Ward, the distinguished naturalist & scientist of Rochester, N.Y."

tickets to the variety of attractions he promoted during his life.

But this is just the sensational listing of P. T. Barnum's glitz. It's his grit and breadth that manifests New England's nineteenth-century promise and opportunity. Barnum ran for Congress and lost to another, unrelated, Barnum, but he served in the Connecticut Assembly. He was mayor of Bridgeport, deeply loved the city, and went bankrupt trying to develop it. As mayor he closed Bridgeport's whorehouses and made a great deal of money promoting morality plays, including a temperance drama that reflected his own tee-totaling, prohibitionist abstemiousness, *The Drunkard*. He wanted to abolish the death penalty, and despite technically owning Joice Heth until her death, he was a staunch advocate of equal rights, including voting rights for African Americans after the Civil War.

He was a trustee of Tufts University, where Jumbo became the school mascot and where the name is still used by its athletic teams. He built a crazily elaborate home in Bridgeport named Iranistan, where he lived with his first and second wife until he died.

Barnum never said, "There's a sucker born every minute," but he did say, "The people like to be humbugged," including himself. He requested, and received, his obituary in the *New York Sun* several years before his death and was delighted at its full accounting.

Henry Ward Beecher and the Beecher Brand

From leaving England, to revolting from its control, ending slavery, gaining the vote for women, and ultimately banning alcohol, the puritanical arc of New England is almost fully crystallized in the Beecher family.

The New Haven Beechers welcomed Lyman (the Lyman Beecher who fathered Harriet Beecher Stowe) into the world in 1775. As a young man he was inspired by the second wave of the Great Awakening and by Yale president Timothy Dwight, who called on Beecher to conduct his Presbyterian ministry as a revival mission.

From Connecticut to Boston, Lyman ascended the ladder of bigger and more prominent churches to become a controversial advocate of temperance in Boston, where drinking was just one of the pastimes that Calvinists like Beecher saw as separating people from God. His ministry went west in 1832, where he felt his zeal could save the entire country from "Catholics and infidels."

The ten surviving Beecher children had lives that were inexorably influenced by their father's radical Christian expression, but their

Henry Ward Beecher, brother to Harriet Beecher Stowe, was a reformist, abolitionist, phrenologist, minister, and supporter of temperance and women's suffrage. He even supported Darwin's theory of evolution. Before the Civil War, Beecher spoke on behalf of and raised money for the abolitionist movement and used the money to send rifles to abolitionists fighting slavery in the Kansas Territory. Later in life he was the first president of the American Woman Suffrage Association. This photograph was taken in 1871.

impact was greatly extended by education at Yale, Bowdoin, Amherst, and Dartmouth, and by creating Hartford Female Seminary.

While virtually all had incredibly productive and interesting lives, two of Lyman Beecher's children had unique impacts on American culture. Henry Ward Beecher was one of the youngest of the Beecher offspring. After graduating from Amherst College, he followed his father west to become head of the Lane Theological Seminary in Ohio, then serving in the Presbyterian Church, first in 1837 in Indiana, then Brooklyn, New York. Though he evolved his father's "new school" theology in writing and lectures, it was in full-throated embrace of morally prescribed activism in politics that catapulted him into celebrity status. As it was for the rest of pre–Civil War New England, the central theme of the Beecher family focus was abolition of slavery.

Beecher sent weapons to radicals like John Brown, who led the first armed conflict in opposition to slavery at Harpers Ferry, Virginia. The weapons used to kill proslavery by law-abiding citizens were called "Beecher's Bibles."

Beecher also raised money to purchase slaves in order to free them. He became quite political in lobbying for outlawing slavery in any new states and western territories. He was devoted to Abraham Lincoln, and Lincoln returned the positive regard, as did Mark Twain and Walt Whitman. Beecher was dubbed "the most famous man in America" because of his uniquely effective impact on both the soul and governance of his country.

His lectures in England helped keep them from allying with the Confederacy and prolonging the war. After the Civil War, Beecher advocated for the immediate and full reinstatement of the Confederacy as part of the Union.

Henry Ward Beecher preached that cutting-edge science— Darwin's theory of natural selection—be applied to society, and that the new power elite of the Industrial Age's ascendant wealthy men was the fittest of our culture and should lead it. He was against unionization, but also against restrictive immigration laws.

> *Beecher was dubbed "the most famous man in America" because of his uniquely effective impact on both the soul and governance of his country.*

Scandals and controversies followed Beecher's later years, involving
alleged affairs, aggressive commercialization of his preaching, and the
co-opting of his "gospel of love" into the "free love" movement of the
1960s.

Invention

Samuel Colt: Of Onions and Magic Carpets

Buildings inevitably reflect their eras and their builders, regardless of,
or despite, original intentions. In Hartford two buildings a quarter mile
apart on the west side of Interstate 91, built 150 years apart, are shin-
ing examples of hubris and cultural evolution.

The onion dome of Colt Armory in Hartford.

When Samuel Colt built his Coltsville gun factory in Hartford in 1855, he wanted his building to embody the verve and energy that made his weaponry the industry leader. Brick was the exterior material of choice, and rectangular was the necessary shape, as were all the openings.

How do you make a sea of brick boxes memorable? Add a startling spice to the brown stew, in this case onion—as in an electric super-glossy blue onion dome, flecked with gilt stars and topped with a gold exclamation point of a rampant colt.

This was nineteenth-century architectural branding at its best: ornament gone wild in contrast to the unrelenting utilitarianism of these new-fangled things called factories. Colt wanted people at ground level to see his icon from afar, like a church steeple, and know that Coltsville had a center, a singular point of reference that was Colt Manufacturing.

After the Civil War Northern and Southern manufacturers were eclipsed by even cheaper manufacturing from abroad. Although it still sells to the military, a lack of war led Colt to file for bankruptcy in June 2015, from which it emerged in January 2016.

The symbolism of the reinhabited nineteenth-century factory buildings becoming the Coltsville National Historical Park is undeniable, now that the long-gone way of life is cast in amber. The Colt Gateway redevelopment project uses public funding and entrepreneurial energy akin to Samuel Colt's to combine apartments, a school, and space for businesses, hopefully reanimating the dead husks of the sprawling old factory complex into economic revival.

Colt Gateway's crowning symbol, the same queerly anomalous onion dome, is now completely restored to glistening beauty. Its impact has been magnified by its eye-level status for millions of cars every year whizzing past it north and south on Interstate 91, the kind of promotional beacon than Samuel Colt would have sought.

The East Armory building of the Colt Firearms Factory in Hartford. Visible from miles away, the highly visible metal star-spangled dome rises above it.

John Deere: The Soil Makes the Man

John Deere was born into an early nineteenth-century Vermont farming community. His dad, William, left for England in 1808 to claim an inheritance, only to, presumably, die at sea, because he was never heard from again.

Without a breadwinner, the Deere family was poor, and John went to the "common schools" in Middlebury, perhaps up to a grammar-school level. By his early teens he was apprenticed to a tanner, where he had a miserable life grinding bark in exchange for a pair of shoes and a suit of clothes.

Deere was drawn to prosperous blacksmith Captain Benjamin Lawrence, who mentored the fatherless Deere for four years, until Deere could become a journeyman and seek his own fortune as a blacksmith. Eventually, John decided to build his own shop. Using borrowed money he bought land and built—twice, because his first shop went up in flames, as did his second, which is unsurprising given the nature of blacksmithing.

Without a shop, and living on borrowed money that was being called due, Deere decided to move west to find work as a blacksmith.

At his new home in Moline, Illinois, Deere began receiving regular visits from other New Englanders. The light iron plows used in New England worked fine in the thin river valley soil of the Northeast but would regularly break in the heavy soil of Illinois. In addition, the blades' rough surface had to be continuously cleaned as it created furrows, making plowing a very frustrating task. A lesser man would see a future in continuous repair, but Deere saw opportunity in fixing the problem, not the blades.

Steel was the answer. Spotting a broken steel saw blade, Deere fashioned that then-rare material into a new kind of blade. From his forge Deere produced a sharp, polished, tough plow blade set into a metal yoke, which was more easily pushed through the sod. The design was a success, ensuring that the blade was cleaned of the cloying soil while plowing. Thus, the steel plow was invented.

From producing three blades in 1838 to one hundred in 1841, Deere had to take on partners to grow the business and to purchase the high-tech British steel that was hard to find in the United States. At this point, production exploded to 1,600 plows in 1850. Deere invented the Hawkeye Riding Cultivator, which relied solely on old-school horse-power. The town of Moline, grew up around his business. His eldest son, Charles, took over the business when it became Deere and Company in 1868.

Deere had nine children and he pulled back from the business during his last twenty years. He founded a bank, involved himself in

A portrait of the older and very successful John Deere.

An 1899 photograph by George Tingley is titled "Spring Ploughing."

his church, and became Moline's mayor as a progressive old-school abolitionist-and-temperance Yankee in out-west Illinois. While you can take the man out of New England, you cannot take New England out of the man.

Robert H. Goddard: Launched from Massachusetts

The father of space flight, Robert Goddard, invented and launched the first liquid-fuel rocket in 1926. Goddard held 214 patents.

Robert H. Goddard started life in the nineteenth century, twenty years before the Wright brothers' first flight, but his work changed the trajectory of the twentieth century. Born in 1882 in Worcester, Massachusetts, he stayed in town for his education earning a B.S. in physics from Worcester Polytechnic Institute and a PhD from Clark University.

Maybe it was Goddard's protracted convalescence from a childhood disease (perhaps caused by overprotective parents nurturing their one surviving child) that allowed Goddard the time to be inspired by his early reading of H. G. Wells's *War of the Worlds* and Jules Verne's *From the Earth to the Moon*. With those fantastic musings in the background of his mind, a cherry tree set him thinking: "On the afternoon of October 19, 1899, I climbed a tall cherry tree. . . It was one of the quiet, colorful afternoons of sheer beauty which we have in October in New England, and as I looked towards the fields at the east, I imagined how wonderful it would be to make some device which had even the possibility of ascending to Mars. I was a different boy when I descended the tree from when I ascended, for existence at last seemed very purposive."

This launched a life of productive science. By the end of his life, Goddard was responsible for more than two hundred patents and had forced the practical application of technology in propulsion that ultimately allowed man to reach beyond his planet. In 1926 Goddard launched the first successful flight of a liquid-propelled rocket in nearby Auburn, Massachusetts. For the rest of his life, Goddard's mission, which initially found little support, transformed the tools of science, exploration, and warfare.

Charles Goodyear: Invention as Salvation

Born in 1800, in New Haven, Connecticut, Charles Goodyear was a classic nineteenth-century New Englander. Like so many of his successful contemporaries, Goodyear was born into business, not farming. But business cuts both ways, and in 1830 the family hardware business went bankrupt.

Rather than find employment in a safer venue, Goodyear saw opportunity in the failures of india rubber. The latex milky sap imported from Brazil was amazingly waterproof, flexible, and useful, unless it became too hot, at which point it liquefied, or became too cold, when it broke into pieces. The material's extreme promise and fatal flaws drove Goodyear to dedicate most of his thirties to stabilizing a product whose limitations wrecked its worth.

Goodyear was a Christian who relied on the wisdom found in the Book of Job to get through a decade of failure until his unyielding focus found reward. Finally, Goodyear combined sulfur with rubber. A high-heat process he dubbed "vulcanizing" (celebrating Vulcan, the Roman god of fire) stabilized the material, at which point his business was on a roll. He patented the process in 1844. From then on Goodyear spent much of his time and money defending his patent and bringing a total of thirty-two infringement cases. In 1852 he hired then secretary of state Daniel Webster to represent him and won a

An undated nineteenth-century portrait of Charles Goodyear.

permanent injunction against any other infringements. Nevertheless, Goodyear died in 1860, $200,000 in debt.

But recognition of Goodyear's extreme commitment to finding a way to make rubber a material that fulfilled its potential came in 1898, when the Goodyear Tire and Rubber Company of Akron, Ohio, was named in his honor.

John Hays Hammond: His Castle Was His Home

Gloucester is a medieval cathedral city in England whose name was formed from the ancient Anglo-Saxon word for fort. Gloucester, Massachusetts, has a medieval fort built in the previous century because its builder fell in love with those castles while spending time in England as a child.

Hammond Castle was built by John Hays Hammond Jr., a scientific genius and quirky thinker. Hammond had one foot in the nineteenth century, but his groundbreaking insights are used today to provide the basis for the technologies that explode all around us today as we Bluetooth, podcast, and download. He had four hundred patented devices, most developed in his nearby radio research laboratory.

Hammond, born to a wealthy West Coast family, figured out how to effectively use radio waves in his twenties. Instead of living large on the left coast, Hammond surfed the vibe of the Roaring Twenties to build his own full-blown castle from 1922 to 1929. It was not so much a mansion as a museum to be lived in, providing the display of his extensive medieval, Roman, and Renaissance collections, as did any number of his contemporaries. Guests included John D. Rockefeller,

Yale University graduate John Hays Hammond Jr. developed methods of electronic remote control used extensively in missiles and torpedoes. Later in life he built a castle in Gloucester, Massachusetts, which is today a museum.

the Barrymores (who, naturally, performed Shakespeare), Greta Garbo, and Cole Porter. There was the in-house pipe organ, the banqueting hall, and faux shops and armaments, plus all the early twentieth-century manifestations that proved, as F. Scott Fitzgerald said, "the rich are different from you and me." But Hammond took it all one step further.

Clutching a cliff overlooking Gloucester Harbor, the Hammond Castle was home to a great deal of paranormal psycho-scientific experimentation. The skull of a crew member from Columbus's expedition is a prize possession. Hammond colored his pool water to make it seem baby-pool deep, when it was in fact over eight feet deep: Guests completely freaked out as Hammond would intentionally swan dive from a second floor balcony. He used his radio remote-control technology to pilot boats in the harbor, clearly without humans on board, to freak out the locals.

The mid-twentieth century saw explorations of telekinesis, color healing ("chromatherapy"), and extra-sensory perception, plus a fair amount of dabbling in the occult. Upon his death, Hammond's estate passed the home onto the Roman Catholic Church, who sold it to a person who tried to cover the costs of ownership with concerts, ultimately to have the castle become what it was always meant to be a museum of art and eccentricity.

Pierre Lallement: The Frenchman Who Patented the Bicycle in New England

Born in 1843 near Nancy, France, Pierre Lallement, was building baby carriages in his hometown when he saw his first dandy horse, a two-wheeled bicycle-like machine that the rider pushed along, propelling it with his feet.

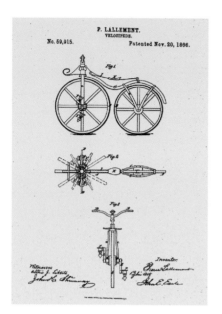

Pierre Lallement bicycle patent, 1866.

But Lallement thought there was a better way. He built a transmission ring—a rotary crank with pedals on the machine's front wheel hub. It's a far cry from the sophistication of today's most generic bicycles, but it kept feet off the ground and hands on the bars. And it conserved more of the rider's energy.

In 1863 Lallement met with the Olivier brothers in Paris. These sons of a wealthy manufacturer saw opportunity and began a factory to build bicycles, but with Pierre Michaux, another early bicycle tinkerer, and not with Lallement. The partnership began to mass-produce the two-wheelers and started a craze in Paris. Lallement may even have worked there.

In 1854 Lallement went to the United States and settled in Ansonia, Connecticut, a manufacturing town on the Housatonic River, where he built an improved bicycle. New Haven's James Carroll provided funding, and Lallement filed America's earliest and only patent application for the pedal bicycle in April 1866; it was awarded that November. Other than the forward wheel hub and pedals, his patent drawing still resembles the dandy horse but with the addition of a thin piece of iron atop the frame that provided both a spring and place for a saddle. It was a much more comfortable riding experience.

A Connecticut manufacturer began cranking out bicycles, but nobody produced Lallement's machine. In 1868 he returned to Paris. In 1880 he went back to the United States to testify on behalf of Albert Pope, a Hartford bicycle maker to whom Lallement had sold his patent rights. He later worked for Pope at a bicycle factory in Brooklyn, where he died at age forty-seven.

Politics

Joshua Lawrence Chamberlain: Marching from Maine to Save the Union

Before the Civil War, Maine was the state furthest from the Mason-Dixon Line and the threat posed by the Confederacy. However, the Civil War was not about physical threats; it was about moral imperatives.

Born in Brewster, Maine, in 1828, Joshua Lawrence Chamberlain thought his career would be in academia—as a professor at Bowdoin College in language and rhetoric, the degrees he received there in 1852, and then studying as an orthodox Congregationalist under Harriet Beecher Stowe's husband, Calvin Stowe, at Bangor Theological Seminary.

When the Civil War broke out, over Bowdoin's objections, Chamberlain enlisted as a lieutenant colonel in the new Twentieth Maine Regiment. The list of Maine's Twentieth Regiment engagements reads like a litany of the bloodiest and most desperate battles of America's bloodiest and most desperate war: Fredericksburg, Chancellorsville, Little Round Top at Gettysburg. Chamberlain gained the Congressional Medal of Honor along with six serious wounds—the last in 1864 nearly fatal.

Returning to Bowdoin after the war, his unending scholarship, writing, and teaching about the war made him a recognized hero. His chivalry was manifest by his order to his men to salute the vanquished Confederate Army as they left, defeated, from Appomattox, where Chamberlain was selected to receive Lee's arms and colors.

Joshua Chamberlain—Maine college professor, war hero, Bowdoin College president, and governor—in his brigadier general uniform. A hero at Gettysburg, Chamberlain received the Medal of Honor.

To Chamberlain, war was not about the bloody brutality but about courage in the belief that, in the hands of Providence, a man's fate was justly realized. Heroism often accrues to public devotion, and Chamberlain was elected governor of Maine four times, and later he helped found the University of Maine at Orono.

Calvin Coolidge: The Last Puritan

Called "The Great Refrainer," "Silent Cal," and "A Puritan in Babylon," John Calvin Coolidge Jr. was born and raised in Vermont. He was the rare leader who gained fame and power by advocating restraint. He was "distinguished for character more than for achievement," noted Democratic presidential candidate Al Smith.

Although young Calvin was shy to the point of oddness, his intelligence and oratory, which he parceled out parsimoniously, became well known at Amherst College, where he became a lawyer. After school, Coolidge moved to Northampton, Massachusetts, where he met the love of his life, Grace Goodhue, who taught at the Clarke School for the Deaf (now the Clarke Schools for Hearing and Speech).

Coolidge set up a law practice in Northampton, where he was first elected councilman, then mayor, then to the Massachusetts legislature, the office of lieutenant governor, and, ultimately, governor of Massachusetts—all the while living in one half of a double rental house.

In every office he held, Coolidge behaved according to his beliefs. In an era when labor unions flexed their muscle to great effect, national attention first came when he fired striking policemen who, he felt, had no right to strike if it endangered the public. The timing was accidentally perfect. In 1920, a divided Republican presidential convention chose Coolidge as Warren Harding's vice-presidential running mate,

President Calvin Coolidge in 1924, a year after the former vice president succeeded Warren G. Harding, who died in office. Coolidge was also elected president in the fall of 1924 in his own right.

trouncing Democratic Ohio governor James M. Cox and running mate
Franklin Delano Roosevelt. This was also the first national election in
which women had the right to vote.

The administration's hands-off, pro-business platform ultimately
led to blatant corruption, including the Teapot Dome scandal. President Harding's fatal heart attack two years into his term gave Coolidge
the presidency. Coolidge's father, a justice of the peace, swore him in
by lamplight in his boyhood hometown of Plymouth Notch, Vermont,
a place still without electricity in 1922.

Coolidge immediately sought out and prosecuted the corruption in
Harding's old administration, cut the federal budget twice, lowered taxes,
and deregulated to the point where the stock market crashed in 1929.

His presidency was full of ironic contrasts between his own New
England asceticism and the freewheeling America of the 1920s. Contemporaries called him "a Scrooge who begat plenty," "the genius of

The Calvin Coolidge residence
at 21 Massasoit Street,
Northampton, Massachusetts.

the average," and a "tortoise reigning over hares." His own successful 1924 campaign slogan was "Keep Cool with Coolidge."

Coolidge publicly advocated for social justice reforms for Native Americans and African Americans, but little was actually done during his administration. He vetoed new veterans benefits but was overridden. Yet Coolidge was not happy with the rigor necessary to be president, declining to run with the classic, flat one-liner: "I do not choose to run for president in 1928." Even though he would have won.

The rest of his party was greatly relieved when he declined another term and his Commerce secretary, Herbert Hoover, ran and won just in time to take the blame for the Great Depression. Like Thomas Jefferson, Coolidge believed that "the government that governs least, governs best." Coolidge's Yankee minimalism was the hard-edged residue of a Puritan foundation.

JFK: Catholic Triumph in a Calvinist Context

A 1961 portrait of President John F. Kennedy.

In New England, Protestants dominated the region for more than two hundred years until 1840. At that time, European economic and political crises sent wave upon wave of Catholic immigrants to America, and very often into Boston.

Into this WASP world the fivefold increase in immigration in the mid-nineteenth century had an immediate reactionary response: the Know-Nothings, an affiliation of nativist Americans who saw immigration as an anti-republican conspiracy by the pope to gain control of Protestant America.

In response, the Democratic Party became the champion of the newly arrived, and the natural consequence was that the Protestant

The house in Brookline, Massachusetts, where Rose and Joseph Kennedy lived and where several of their children, including John F. Kennedy, were born.

"dry" Republican's fervor for Prohibition had a natural counterweight formed in the Catholic "wet" Democrats. Politics played out this counterculture dynamic for the next century.

Into this context came the Kennedy family. All four of Joseph P. Kennedy's grandparents came to America in the 1840s, and his purebred status as a scion of the anti-Brahmin Catholic counter class was secure. After attending Boston Latin high school and Harvard (just like his Brahmin rivals), Joe Kennedy took lucrative advantage of Prohibition's end in 1933. Never the creator or inventor, he was an investor and financial strategist and became one of America's twenty richest people by the mid-twentieth century.

Money and politics are intimate bedfellows, and Joe, emboldened by Catholic Al Smith's run in 1928, decided his eldest son, Joseph P. Kennedy Jr., would be a great United State president. But that son, like too many of that generation, was a casualty of World War II. His younger brother, the often sickly John Fitzgerald Kennedy, survived harrowing action to come home a war hero and was thus effectively launched into politics in 1946 at age twenty-nine with an easy win to the US House of Representatives.

But politics and families in New England are inexorably mixed. There was a mirror image to the Kennedy family in Massachusetts: The Lodges were descended from the Cabots, who came ashore to New England in 1680 as one of the signature Brahmin families.

The same year that John F. Kennedy was elected to the US House of Representatives, another WW II vet, Henry Cabot Lodge Jr., was reelected to the US Senate, having quit to fight in the war. Also part of the Harvard club, Lodge was not just a political veteran but Massachusetts political royalty: His grandfather, two great-great-grandfathers, and a great-great-great-grandfather all had been US senators.

As if pulled on a collision course by the gravitational density of each other's political, religious, and cultural differences, John Fitzgerald Kennedy and Henry Cabot Lodge Jr. politically crashed into each other twice: first in 1952, where the Boston Irish boy wonder took the Boston Brahmin's Senate seat. Later, as if a final exclamation point was needed, JFK and Lyndon Johnson eked out a tight win against Richard Nixon and Lodge in 1960's presidential race.

Kennedy went on to become a fully romanticized hero—he of the Purple Heart, Pulitzer Prize, superstar spouse, and fellow senator brothers Bobby and Ted (who, incidentally defeated Henry Cabot Lodge Jr.'s son George for his Senate seat in 1962!).

All those larger-than-life effusions of glory were but a halo around JFK's hallowed status as the youngest president elected and then to die in office, assassinated at no small cost to the most powerful nation on earth. His Catholicism meant nothing to America at his death.

"Ask not what your country can do for you, ask what you can do for your country" may just as easily have been spoken by New Englanders Nathan Hale or Benjamin Franklin (or Franklin's import, Thomas Paine). Perhaps the transition of our cultural spirituality will ultimately fall away from Calvinist or Catholic roots—but never from the full-throated devotion to a greater good.

The Arts

Louisa May Alcott: Industrious Wordsmith

"I will make a battering ram of my head and make my way through this rough world." These are the words of fifteen-year-old Louisa May Alcott, written in 1847.

To be a talented, driven woman in the nineteenth century was to be either frustrated or renegade. Alcott was wildly successful playing by the rules that limited women in her time, but her family's radical New England-based beliefs empowered her to assault the "rough world" she encountered in New England.

"I'll be rich and famous and happy before I die, see if I won't!" she asserted.

Educated by her father, grounded by her Christian mother, then launched into any number of moneymaking endeavors, including looking after Emerson offspring, were all good. But writing was Louisa's

A portrait of Louisa May Alcott in the 1870s.

"I'll be rich and famous and happy before I die, see if I won't!" she asserted.

gift, and whether using the name Flora Fairfield or A. M. Bernard, the poems, potboilers, and humorous essays (including one based on the failed commune) all got published. When she became a nurse during the Civil War, she wrote about that as well.

Her break was the recounting of her family's active life with the wildly successful 1868 publication of *Little Women*, followed by lesser successes, but all made the money and brought the fame Louisa so earnestly sought as a child.

Her tomboy adventurism translated into a can-do attitude in adulthood, which helped her cope after one sister died of scarlet fever and another left for marriage. Although she never married, she parented

Right and facing page: Louisa May Alcott's home in Concord, Massachusetts, where she wrote *Little Women*.

one sister's child and adopted a nephew. Her humor was evident, and her energy was unrelenting.

Although her first and abiding concern was earning a living, her political efforts were classic nineteenth-century progressive: abolition, temperance, women's rights, and suffrage advocate. This last cause brought a unique New England success. Forty years before the nation caught up to her town's forward ways, Louisa was able to vote in a local school-board election before she died.

As a nurse in the Civil War, where illness killed more soldiers than bullets, she discovered that nurses were not immune. Alcott got typhoid pneumonia that was "treated" with mercury-laced calomel, a poison that permanently affected her health until her death, two days after the death of her father, whom she essentially supported for his last thirty years.

Ralph Waldo Emerson: Transcending Religion

The Emerson family came to the New World in 1635, and it soon became a family extending its tree deep into the religious roots of seventeenth-century New England.

That unrelenting reminders of mortality (in the deaths of his father, siblings, wife, and son) led Ralph Waldo Emerson to reject Christianity in a place, New England, that had been the refuge for its most extreme seventeenth-century adherents.

But Emerson was not simply a rebel rejectionist—he sought enlightenment in his connections to William Wadsworth and Thomas Carlyle, and found inspiration, with others, in the Romanticist movement—including the writings of Samuel Taylor Coleridge. Emerson was Henry David Thoreau's mentor and embraced Thoreau's focus on nature as a key to spiritual fulfillment.

Although named "The Sage of Concord" because of his thoughtful and original writing, Emerson had intellectual detractors as well. Herman Melville, Nathaniel Hawthorne, and others could not approve of Emerson's rejection of "evil" as an independent force. Rather than "good" and "evil," Emerson and others offered the idea that each human is, in fact, a manifestation of the divine order of the natural world—a philosophy dubbed transcendentalism. Emerson transcended the applications of religiosity and ritual and creating perhaps the first New Age spirituality fully 120 years before the 1960s. Fusing John Locke, Goethe, Unitarianism, and ultimately atheism, Emerson believed in the natural good of all creation as perceived and embraced by each person.

In his long life he traveled extensively; collected a large library of Chinese, Indian, and Persian texts; and lectured over 1,500 times, becoming as successful as any driven industrialist, even though the transcendentalist movement wanted to replace money with moral insight: "A man is fed, not that he may be fed, but that he may work," wrote Emerson in his treatise *Nature* in 1836.

In the wake of the American Revolution, the intellectual reset from "under God and king" to each person's right to "life, liberty, and the pursuit of happiness" had sweeping, resonant economic, cultural, and spiritual implications. It was a time when the environmental landscape of New England transitioned from family-based subsistence farming and artisanal craft-based commodities into the advent of the Industrial Revolution. It was not surprising that Emerson and the transcendentalists hated slavery not as an affront to God's will but for stealing each man's divinity—"the divine sufficiency of the individual" made every slave into a martyr of violated divinity.

Ralph Waldo Emerson, the poet, essayist, and transcendentalist, photographed about 1884.

Ralph Waldo Emerson bought this house, named "Bush," in 1835. Over the years he expanded and updated it and added more land to the property. Off the central hall is Emerson's study, the place where he wrote many of his best-known works. When Edward, Emerson's son, died in 1930, the house was taken over by the Ralph Waldo Emerson Memorial Association.

When Oliver Wendell Holmes Sr. heard Emerson's speech "The American Scholar" in 1837, reflecting a complete rethinking of New England's religious legacy, he called it "America's Intellectual Declaration of Independence."

Emily Dickinson: The Beauty within Enigma

Born into a classic New England family of seventeenth-century Calvinists and nineteenth-century lawyers, academics, and politicians, Emily Dickinson and her life are as compelling as her poetry for the same reason: mystery.

Dickinson never married, seldom ventured out of the family residence—the Homestead—and never wanted to express her brilliance beyond her intimates. This may be due to trauma. In a letter from April 1862, she wrote, "I had a terror since September, I could tell to none; and so I sing, as the boy does by the burying ground, because I am afraid." Or it may have been that single and at home is the way she wished to live. People, she noted in a letter, "talk of hallowed things aloud—and embarrass my Dog—He and I don't object to them if they'll exist on their side."

And in poetry she wrote, "The Soul selects her own Society— Then—shuts the Door."

In the light of twenty-first-century feminism and psychological insight, today's reading paints a picture of a woman of extraordinary brilliance out of step with her cultural time and place, while fully enmeshed in her immediate family.

She was deeply engaged with her sister, Lavinia ("Vinnie"); and her brother, Austin; and sister-in-law, Susan Gilbert Dickinson. She also had a long passionate correspondence with pious author Thomas Wentworth Higginson, and may have been considered becoming engaged to a widowed friend of her father. She was deeply attached to a Philadelphia preacher and totally adored her dog. But she never committed to anything as much as she did to her lifelong devotion to the written word.

Dickinson had physical symptoms of her emotional distress. She was treated in Cambridge for two long periods for iritis, severe pain and inflammation in both eyes. On her death in 1886 from Bright's disease (today also called kidney nephritis), her doctor said it was due to the accumulation of stress. After Emily's death Vinnie found Emily's poems, read them, and proceeded to see that they were published.

Portrait of Emily Dickinson made about 1894.

The Emily Dickinson House in Amherst, Massachusetts, built 1856.

Dickinson's body of work contained almost 1,800 poems and hundreds of letters. In 1890 *The Poems of Emily Dickinson* was published.

It took seventy years to finally get a full, uncompromised compilation of her unaltered words in print. Scholarship triumphed over editing, and Dickinson's language rings like a bell amid the foggy particulars of her complicated isolation.

Unlike Harriet Beecher Stowe or Henry Wadsworth Longfellow, who became rich and famous by their words, Dickinson had fully assumed her life's work was hers and hers alone. She created an intricate system of punctuation and lineation. Some contemporary feminists interpret Dickinson's presentation of herself largely as a rejection of patriarchal authority. Others see a dysfunctional manic-depressive.

No matter the motivation or complications, the brilliance of her craft has far outlasted her more celebrated contemporaries. Finding value in self-expression may simply be human, but the bold belief in its power has a safe harbor in New England, then and now.

Daniel Chester French: Freeze Framing in New England

Born in Exeter, New Hampshire, sculptor Daniel Chester French's early life itinerary reads like a New England train schedule: He also lived in Cambridge, Massachusetts, then two years in Florence, Italy, followed by a return to Massachusetts (first Amherst, and finally Concord). The ride ended when French built his summer studio in Stockbridge, Massachusetts, where he came to spend six months of the year "in heaven," by his account.

Like many nineteenth-century artists, French (after a brief stint at MIT) apprenticed with several greats, including William Morris Hunt,

The statue *Minute Man* adjacent to the North Bridge at the Minute Man National Historical Park in Concord, Massachusetts.

John Quincy Adams Ward, and Abigail May Alcott. His extremely evocative and realistically romantic sculptures reflect his classical training in Florence. In the full flower of his career, French waged a lifelong competition with New Yorker Augustus Saint-Gaudens for the cream of the civic, institutional, and private commissions that trumpeted America's heroes in the period of high Beaux-Arts.

The young sculptor became a New England point of pride in 1874 when he was commissioned by the family of Ralph Waldo Emerson to

Daniel Chester French's studio, Chesterwood, in Stockbridge, Massachusetts, where he made the seven-foot model of Abraham Lincoln that was used by Piccirilli Brothers to carve the nineteen-foot-tall statue that resides, thoughtfully, inside the Lincoln Memorial in Washington, D.C. The statue took twenty-eight blocks of Georgia marble; French made the final adjustments to the memorable work of art.

create the sculpture *Minute Man*, set at his hometown Concord's North Bridge, site of the "shot heard round the world." The rakish projection of revolutionary resolve embodied in a solitary no-nonsense New Englander captured the revolutionary spirit of the original colonies.

Pride may goeth before a fall, but it keeps sculptors pretty busy. Sculptures by French became the focal art form for scores of extraordinary public and institutional buildings—including his Arts and Sciences creations at Boston Public Library, *Alma Mater* at Low Library at Columbia University, *John Harvard Monument* at (you guessed it) Harvard, *The Four Continents* at the US Custom House—climaxing in perhaps the most evocative sculpture of American history, the Olympian capture of Abraham Lincoln in Henry Bacon's temple to the Great Emancipator in Washington, D.C.

Nathaniel Hawthorne: The Puritan's Hangover

Seventeenth-century New England was not a tolerant place. Nathaniel Hawthorne, a nineteenth-century man, was acutely aware of the extremity of the state religion's impact on seventeenth-century society and spent a lifetime creating parables of imposed and revealed morality and sin in New England. Hawthorne's fictional works were partly inspired by the shame he felt for the crimes committed by his intolerant ancestors.

His sea captain father died of yellow fever on a voyage in 1808, when Hawthorne was four. His mother soldiered on with the help of her brothers. When young Nathaniel badly injured his leg, he was forced to remain immobile for months and so discovered a passion for reading. This pursuit led him to Bowdoin College in Maine. After

Author Nathaniel Hawthorne in the 1860s.

graduation, Hawthorne bucked the Calvinist work ethic of his forefathers. He came home to live with his mother for a dozen years, writing and self-publishing more than earning a living, an attitude clearly evident when Hawthorne noted, "I do not want to be a doctor and live by men's diseases, nor a minister to live by their sins, nor a lawyer and live by their quarrels. So, I don't see that there is anything left for me but to be an author."

Relatively late in life, in 1842, he married painter Sophia Peabody, a marriage that was only possible once his writing had enough proven success to demonstrate his suitability for her hand. Their loving union resulted in three children in quick succession. Sophia's devotion to the non-Christian transcendentalist movement gave Nathaniel an alternative to his lifelong faith. She also married into Hawthorne's connections with fellow writers Louisa May Alcott, Ralph Waldo Emerson, and Herman Melville, who made Hawthorne reconsider some of his depressing seventeenth-century morality tales—for a time.

His focus on morality struck gold in 1850 when *The Scarlet Letter* was published amid a transitional New England culture. The story was the classic New England allegorical morality play set in the extreme Christian state that Hawthorne's ancestors occupied. Meanwhile, the Great Awakening faded and the Industrial Revolution offered the new technology of mass-printing. Books published quickly and sold fairly cheaply allowed *The Scarlet Letter* to brew a perfect storm of past, present, and cutting-edge meaning. Symbolism and allegory resonate only when they are based in realities. The Puritan hangover lasted in New England even after the Civil War, when New Hampshire ended its state-supported religion in 1877.

Hawthorne was buried in 1864 on Author's Ridge in the Sleepy Hollow Cemetery in Concord, near his literary friends the Alcotts, Emerson, and Thoreau. The angst over original sin, good and evil, the deity of Christ, and the soul of man all lay to rest in a slowly secularizing part of America, where the afterlife has more to do with legacies than with heaven or hell.

Winslow Homer: "When I Have Selected the Thing Carefully, I Paint It Exactly as It Appears"

Recognized as America's greatest representational painter of the nineteenth century, Winslow Homer's stark allegories in art followed a path that started and finished in New England.

He was born in 1836, in then-rural Cambridge, Massachusetts, to Charles and Henrietta Homer. Winslow's father was an entrepreneur and had two points of influence in his life. He first pushed his talented son to answer an ad for a lithography apprenticeship in New York City that connected young Winslow to that art world. Secondly, Charles Homer's failed attempts at the hardware business, finding gold in California, and raising capital in Europe made Winslow Homer's dad often absent from family life.

Those absences made Winslow all the closer to his mother, Henrietta, who was not only a watercolorist but also had the grit, humor, and focus of a Swamp Yankee, making a family work while the father was off on the next get-rich-quick scheme. With his mother's talent and dry perspective, the country boy

Homer's "Painting Room," which he added to his studio in 1890.

Second floor of Homer's studio.

Painter Winslow Homer's 1884 studio in Prouts Neck, Maine.

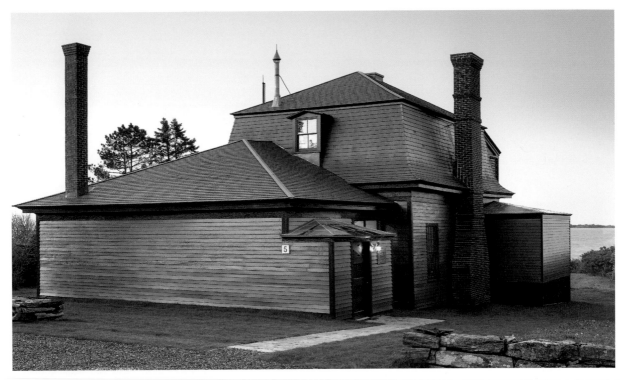

Winslow Homer's studio, the exterior view from the west side.

The parlor.

The studio fireplace.

Winslow spent his childhood continuing self-education in the fine arts, a personal devotion that carried through his time in New York. After a decade, Homer rejected the virtues of steady money for the potentials of manifesting his own destiny: "From the time I took my nose off that lithographic stone I have had no master, and never shall have any." He perhaps sounded a bit like Dad, whom Winslow cared for after his mother died.

Before he went off on his own, Homer went to the Civil War as an artist for *Harper's Weekly*, depicting the daily life of soldiers and also experiencing the terrors of war and its completely unromantic realities of death and fear. Those cold truths informed the underlying emotional starkness found in his later work.

When he returned to his New York studio after the war, he began to have some success as an artist and joined a group of New York writers and artists who called themselves the Tile Club, where he became known as "the Obtuse Bard." His painting life allowed him to meet Helena de Kay and to place her, repeatedly, in his paintings. The seven surviving letters from Homer to de Kay from the period indicate that his lifelong bachelorhood may have had its roots in the unrequited regard for his muse and was the cause for his relentless isolation in creating his art.

Homer always let the physical context of his experience inform his painting. Homer spent the almost obligatory year in Paris in 1867, painting the peasant life he encountered. He spent time absorbing the life of former slaves in Virginia and then travelled to the English village of Cullercoats to capture the coastal fishing life. His seminal influence, which saw Homer decide to abandon the New York art scene and return full time to an extreme New England life, was his move to Prouts Neck, Maine, in 1883. There he lived and worked for the next twenty-seven years until his death.

Ship-Building, Gloucester Harbor, 1873.

Hauling in the Nets, 1887.

Those years saw his art fully flesh out, allowing his representations of the unbridled power of nature manifest in storm-tossed seas, of human vulnerability, and of humble survival in a rough world. All of this was almost puritanical in its veneration of the stoic New England coastal life. Contemporaries came to call him the "Yankee Robinson Crusoe" and a "hermit with a brush," as his isolation in Prouts Neck was year-round, save for summer trips to the Adirondacks.

Ultimately, Homer found financial success, but only late in life as the public began to pay attention to his great contemporary critical acclaim. His frugality was well known, but despite it, he did receive help in the tough years from his affluent brother Charles. Financial security and the death of the father (who Homer had cared for during his father's last years) made Homer's last dozen years a valedictory of artistic excellence.

Despite all hopes at sophistication, New England is essentially defined by the rough edges of its landscape, climate, and original descendants. Homer felt the authenticity of those raw realities and brought them home in art that was both unflinching and beautifully rendered—much like the aesthetic essence of New England itself.

Julia Ward Howe: What Would We Be Without That Song?

She was born in 1819 and died in 1910, a life bracketed by the fullness of American nineteenth-century evolution, a world that moved from whale oil lamps and buggies to electric power, motorcars, and telephones. And from slavery to freedom.

Ward was born in New York City, the daughter of a Wall Street banker and a poet. Ward's mother died when she was still young and so her father assumed responsibility for raising the children with a dominant hand.

Because of the family's status and wealth, Julia met and got to know literary celebrities of her day, such as Charles Dickens and Henry Wadsworth Longfellow, mostly thanks to her brother Sam, who opened her eyes to the creative personalities of the day (she later became friends with Mark Twain, Oscar Wilde, and William Dean Howells). In 1839, when her father died, she moved into his big Manhattan house. Sam recently had married Emily Astor, John Jacob Astor's granddaughter. Emily took the two under her wings and led them into the world of New York's highest society. Sadly, in 1841 Emily Astor died during childbirth, leaving Sam, and the other sisters again in mourning.

Two years later, Julia was introduced to Dr. Samuel Gridley Howe, or "Chev," an intellectual and activist for prison reform and educating

BATTLE HYMN OF THE REPUBLIC.

BY MRS. JULIA WARD HOWE.

Mine eyes have seen the glory of the coming of the Lord:
He is trampling out the vintage where the grapes of wrath
   are stored;
He hath loosed the fateful lightnings of His terrible swift sword:
      His truth is marching on.
  CHORUS—Glory, glory, hallelujah!
      Glory, glory, hallelujah!
      Glory, glory, hallelujah!
        His truth is marching on.

I have seen Him in the watch-fires of a hundred circling camps;
They have builded Him an altar in the evening dews and
   damps:
I can read His righteous sentence by the dim and flaring lamps:
      His day is marching on.
  CHORUS—Glory, glory, hallelujah, &c.
      His day is marching on.

I have read a fiery gospel writ in burnished rows of steel:
"As ye deal with my contemners, so with you my grace shall
   deal;
Let the Hero, born of woman, crush the serpent with his heel,
      Since God is marching on."
  CHORUS—Glory, glory, hallelujah &c.
      Since God is marching on.

He has sounded forth the trumpet that shall never call retreat:
He is sifting out the hearts of men before His judgment seat:
Oh, be swift, my soul, to answer Him! be jubilant my feet!
      Our God is marching on!
  CHORUS—Glory, glory, hallelujah, &c.
      Our God is marching on!

In the beauty of the lilies Christ was born across the sea,
With a glory in His bosom that transfigures you and me;
As he died to make men holy, let us die to make men free,
      While God is marching on.
  CHORUS—Glory, glory, hallelujah, &c.
      While God is marching on.

Published by the Supervisory Committee for Recruiting Colored Regiments

Born in 1819 and shown here in 1908, Julia Ward Howe was the first woman elected to the American Academy of Arts and Letters. Later in life she turned her intelligence and considerable energy toward women's rights, prison reform, and sex education.

"Battle Hymn of the Republic," written by Julia Ward Howe, was published first in *Atlantic Monthly* in 1862 "by the Supervisory Committee for Recruiting Colored Regiments" for the Civil War.

the blind who was nearly twice her age. In 1843 they married and two years later they moved to Boston.

During their marriage, Ward's husband expected her to behave like the proper and submissive model wife of the mid-nineteenth century. But she wrote poetry, published a collection of her poems, and fought with her husband over her right to expression. She also got involved in abolition and women's rights.

Although her husband continued to disapprove of Julia's writing, she did it anyway. In 1861, when "Battle Hymn of the Republic" was published, Julia became a celebrity. By 1876, Julia had a well-established career as a woman's rights promoter, poet, and reformer.

After her husband died, Julia discovered that his bad investments had left her both a widow and relatively poor, and she wrote in her journal, "Start my new life today." She spent the rest of her life writing fiction and children's books and supporting causes such as women's suffrage.

Charles Ives: New Music from New England

Charles Ives, born in 1874 in Danbury, Connecticut, created uniquely American and profoundly innovative music. The verve, drive, humor, and rigor of his voluminous compositions throughout the first half of the twentieth century confounded traditionalists and delighted the rest of us.

His father, George Ives, served as the Union Army's youngest bandmaster during the Civil War and returned home to become a professional musician in Danbury, which he helped dub "the most musical city in America." Ives began composing at the age of thirteen. By age fourteen Charles became the youngest salaried church organist in Connecticut (of which there were many).

Ives began studying music when very young and learned much from his father, George, a Civil War bandmaster. His father was a musical experimentalist, a passion that his son picked up and used to make a career as a composer.

His immersion in the musical factory town of Danbury naturally brought a tasty vernacular flavor to his musical offerings. "The Going on the Hook and Ladder" echoed firemen's parades. "From Steeples and the Mountains" is fraught with memories of Danbury church bells.

He attended Hopkins School, then Yale. He offered up his music skills to any venue he could, including becoming organist for Center Church on the New Haven green as a freshman—the top religious music job in New Haven. He loved parties and ragtime and composed "Here's to Good Old Yale"—a fitting testament to his love of Old Blue.

Charles Ives embodied the energy of New England's hustling, bustling Yankee entrepreneurial legacy in his music. He explored virtually every format imaginable: vocal, small ensemble, band, and orchestra.

In 1906 the peripatetic Ives suffered a physical and emotional break, likely a stress-induced heart attack, and met and married Harmony Twichell, a transcendentalist and intellectual, with whom he adopted two children.

Musicians struggle to earn a living, even one as gifted as Ives, so he started his own insurance firm, Ives & Company, in 1907. It grew into a very successful business. Despite his day job in insurance, he continued an insanely productive musical career.

Though having neither the sentimental or popular appeal of Stephen Foster or Aaron Copland as far as American composers go, Ives was unapologetically American but constitutionally incapable of lapsing into anything predictable or sentimentally soft. His work appeals to musicians because it revels in the possibilities bound up in the sounds and cultural realities of New England life.

"Music is life," he said, being literal in the words he used as it applied to his own. Another heart attack at age forty-four did not immediately slow his pace, but the volume of work did reduce as the twentieth century reached its middle. As his health ebbed, the celebration of his musical work rose, and it peaked in 1947 when he won a Pulitzer Prize for Music.

Henry Wadsworth Longfellow: The Rhyme of His Time

Longfellow's life was in lyric harmony with New England. He was born in 1807, in what is now Portland, Maine, when it was still part of Massachusetts, before the Missouri Compromise balanced the new non-slave state Maine with the new slave state of Missouri in 1820.

Very well educated at Bowdoin and the world tour, Longfellow learned twelve languages and taught some of them at Harvard as the Smith Professor of Modern Languages and of Belle Letters. He quit Harvard when he realized his time was best spent in the all-consuming act of creating poetry. His decision was expedited by his second marriage into a wealthy Boston family—though the marriage ended in tragedy.

His life as a world-celebrated poet centered on easy rhymes born of difficult times, personal and public. His own tragedies were debilitating: one wife died in the miscarriage of their firstborn; a second wife died after setting herself on fire when sealing a letter with candle wax; and of his six children, Fanny died in her second year of life. (Fanny was the first child born in America whose mother received anesthesia during her birth.)

These life-changing pivots were vehicles that Longfellow used to focus his poetic energy. His gift for sing-song rhyme needed an edge to go beyond child's verse. So "Paul Revere's Ride" in 1861 had a clear antislavery message during the Civil War, as did *Poems on Slavery*. Loving

**The Henry Wadsworth
Longfellow statue in
Portland, Maine.**

someone who is dying is captured in *Evangeline*. *The Song of Hiawatha* was dedicated to the Native Americans of early New England.

Complementing his public declarations against slavery was his use of money from his extraordinary publishing success to fund the Underground Railroad.

His commercial success—beyond that of these contemporaries—clearly ushered in a middle-class veneration of the poet's product worldwide. *The Courtship of Miles Standish* sold ten thousand copies in one day in London. His work played the puritanical off the romantic, put the high-minded in bed with the humble, a mixed message reflecting America's aspiring awkward adolescence.

Longfellow's extreme productivity and its commercial success via the new media of his age—mass-printed publications—matched his passion for poetry. His was a full-throated Yankee expression without a tinge of tedium. His several periods of poet's block were each caused by the personal tragedies so typical of the unpredictable life expectancies of the nineteenth century. The extreme fame Longfellow had during his time was wildly distinct from twentieth-century critical derision of his melodic methods.

For New Englanders, usefulness rightfully garnered financial rewards, and Henry Wadsworth Longfellow made poetry meaningful for millions, thus useful in the day-to-day life of Americans, thus a success by any standard.

Samuel Eliot Morison: The Center of the Center of New England

Samuel Eliot Morison is, perhaps, the epicenter for a New England perspective. A historian whose fifty books, fifty years of teaching, two Pulitzer Prizes, and unending academic awards do small justice to his lasting impact. He is as iconic to New England academia as Yastrzemski is to baseball or Orr to hockey.

His work played the puritanical off the romantic, put the high-minded in bed with the humble, a mixed message reflecting America's aspiring awkward adolescence.

Mr. & Mrs. Samuel Morison with John W. McElroy (left) holding a Harvard-Columbus Expedition pennant.
WORLD TELEGRAM & SUN PHOTO BY EDWARD LYNCH.

He was a man with one foot in the nineteenth century (born in 1887) and a mind split between multiple centuries (most often fifteenth, seventeenth, and twentieth).

Morison was one of the period's last Boston Brahmins. Morison ("SEM" to his WASP cohorts) was St. Paul's School, Harvard College, and Oxford University trained. A lifelong Harvard professor, he lived on Brimmer Street in Beacon Hill and has a statue on Commonwealth Avenue (in Boston, of course).

His list of New England writing is amazingly comprehensive. In 1921 he wrote *The Maritime History of Massachusetts, 1783–1860*. In the 1930s he wrote *Builders of the Bay Colony: A Gallery of Our Intellectual Ancestors*, *The Intellectual Life of Colonial New England*, *The Founding of Harvard College*, *Harvard College in the Seventeenth Century*, *Three Centuries of Harvard:*

1636–1936, and *The Puritan Pronaos*. Then, after his prodigious writing on World War II, he went on to *The Ropemakers of Plymouth* and *The Story of the "Old Colony" of New Plymouth* and editing the definitive work by William Bradford, *Of Plymouth Plantation, 1620–1647*. This body of work is amazing enough, but it's more astonishing when you realize his most acclaimed work was in writing about Christopher Columbus and American naval history in World War II.

His unconventional perspective was that, to best write history, you must physically see the facts still left on the ground. He visited Columbus's landing sites and sailed with the American Navy into war. But genetically he was part of the human legacy of every Puritan, Pilgrim, or Harvard figure he devoted his time to understanding and writing about.

In a 1931 essay called "Those Misunderstood Puritans," he, perhaps asking for some relief from stereotyping his own legacy, rejected the idea that "the fathers of New England" were "somber kill-joys." Instead he blamed the stereotype on nineteenth-century Victorian rewriting of facts. Morison posited that "the right approach to the Puritan founders of New England is historical, by way of the Middle Ages. . . They were, broadly speaking, the Englishmen who had accepted the Reformation without the Renaissance."

He was not so much an academic, but a writer who taught. He cared so passionately about his craft that when interrupted by incessant barking of a neighbor's dog while trying to write, he went outside and shot it. He had harsh judgments about the students he was compelled to teach while providing a venue for his writing: ". . . they imagine that the historian's problem is simply to compare points of view and describe trends. It is not." He also was not thrilled with the academic constructions of his peers. He was president of the American Historical Association, an organization whose meetings he rarely attended.

The Samuel Eliot Morison Statue in Boston.

Jill Lepore, professor of American history at Harvard University and chair of Harvard's History and Literature Program, notes in a piece on Morison in *The New Yorker* that "Sam Morison never met a footnote he didn't like, but his relationship to academic history was a complicated one. At Harvard, he was neither a natural teacher nor a beloved one. He never held office hours, he made his students come to class in coat and tie, and he refused to teach Radcliffe girls (he considered them frivolous). He liked to lecture in riding breeches and, in later years, in his Navy uniform."

Historian Bernard Bailyn observes, "There is no 'Morison school.' Because he wrote more for the public than for his fellow-historians, Morison has few academic disciples today, and, if the chain reaction of dullness continues unbroken, Morison is as much to blame as anybody."

But could there be the popularizing tradition of historical writers like David McCullough, Doris Kerns Goodwin, Joseph Ellis, or Jon Meacham without Samuel Eliot Morison showing millions of baby boomer students that fact-based history could be written with literature-level prose?

Frederick Law Olmsted: Eighth-Generation Charm

Frederick Law Olmsted's largely nineteenth-century life was one of extremes. His lineage was extreme New England: eighth-generation Hartford family of substantial, if not showy, assets.

In his youth he developed an extreme disability. At eighteen, just before he was to enter Yale, sumac poisoning of his eyes was so serious that he bowed out of higher education.

A view of the Ladies Pavilion built by Frederick Law Olmsted in New York City's Central Park. According to the park website, "The Pavilion is made from cast iron, slate, wood, and stone and is situated on The Lake at Hernshead, a rock structure that resembles the shape of a heron . . . Coupled with the Pavilion's lakeside location and ample roof, the stone floor makes the Pavilion a cool respite on hot summer days . . . Thick iron poles resplendent with intricate Victorian designs support the roof. The Pavilion measures approximately 9 by 15 feet and weighs about 2 tons."

His temperament, however, remained extremely restless. In his own words, his younger years were "given over to a decently vagabond life, generally pursued under the guise of an angler, a fowler, or a dabbler of the shallowest shores of the deep sea."

His father, John, attempted private tutoring by individual clergy to no great focus, so still in his teens Frederick moved to New York to work in a dry goods store. A series of peripatetic meanderings ensued: dabbling in France, working on a boat to China, attending lectures at Yale.

His father bought him a farm to manage on Staten Island (the house on Hylan Boulevard still stands), but he wouldn't settle. Soon after he opted to be a publisher, often of his own writing, appropriate of his meanders. He and friends walked about England chronicling farms and gardens. Later, he toured various locales in the pre–Civil War South, exposing the evils of slavery, which he wrote about in the *New York Times*, then the *New-York Daily Times*. He co-founded *The Nation* magazine and later the journal *Garden and Forest* before becoming managing editor of *Putnam's Monthly* for its last two years of existence.

He was never lazy, simply a smart and curious student of life. He found writing about the Southern slave states inspiring. Meeting the great architect Andrew Jackson Downing opened up his vision of design, but never led him to alight on a central life mission that unified his desire to write and his passion for design.

Given his own recounting of his character as that of "a wholly unpractical man," it is astonishing that through connections he was able to apply his extraordinary talents in ways that made him truly the greatest landscape designer in the nineteenth century and arguably the greatest in American history. His instant access to huge commissions without formal training or even apprenticeship in design came, bizarrely, from his publishing endeavors.

In 1856, after six months living in London and visiting the Continent and seeing its parks, Olmsted returned to New York. A decade of dabbling in publishing netted him the contacts he needed to apply for and to obtain the job of superintendent of Central Park, after he and his partner, architect Calvert Vaux, won the design competition for the park.

Following this first at-bat home run came more than five hundred commissions, involving the complete design of extensive parks throughout New York, Buffalo, Boston, and San Francisco, and Montreal's Mount Royal. A huge sweep of forty academic institutions from Harvard to Stanford commissioned Olmsted. Additionally hundreds of private estates—including George Vanderbilt's Biltmore—sought out his talents. Civic landscape designs include the US Capitol and the Connecticut State Capitol. An important commission came with the Chicago World's Fair in 1893, where Olmsted had to manage the entire enterprise when the director died before it opened.

The extremity of Olmsted's reach and impact cannot be overstated, all due to his extreme talent and vision. He managed to tap public discomfort with the inhuman scale of the new and huge modern city that was bred of the exploding Industrial Age. His gift also was the clarity of creating places that took the English deer park into a fully composed set of spaces connected by his invention of parkways, broad greenways of transportation that interconnected within each city. His parkways are sweeping, compelling, right for his time, and still fully loved today.

Ultimately, in his late seventies, Olmsted succumbed to chronic dementia and, ironically was effectively committed to a place he had designed: McLean Hospital in Belmont, Massachusetts. As he walked the grounds he had designed, his fully loaded and failing mind yet was able to recount certain features that contractors had omitted: "Confound them!" was his legitimate response.

Harriet Beecher Stowe: The Woman Who Built Uncle Tom's Cabin

If Henry Ward Beecher was a greater-than-life voice of cultural evolution for a liberal reinvention of religion, his sister's life of expression more effectively exploded the worst prejudices that Beecher worked so ardently to overcome. While Harriet Beecher Stowe may have been prohibited from preaching, her voice was heard with unparalleled impact worldwide.

Uncle Tom's Cabin **author Harriet Beecher Stowe was born in Litchfield, Connecticut, schooled in Hartford, moved to Cincinnati in 1832, where her father was president of a seminary, and later met and married Calvin Ellis Stowe, who taught there and was himself a fervent abolitionist.**

Harriet was Henry's slightly older sister, and although all of her brothers became ministers and her younger sister Isabella was a founder of the National Women's Suffrage Association, Harriet had the transformative impact on literature, publishing, the abolitionist movement, and, ultimately, the reality that women had every intellectual and creative component of their male counterparts.

Young Harriet studied a traditional male curriculum at the Litchfield Female Academy. Though she later taught at the Hartford Female Seminary founded by her sister Catharine, her lifelong central passion was writing.

She met her husband, Calvin Ellis Stowe, who was a professor at her father's seminary in Cincinnati. While there she witnessed the transport of slaves, a scene that left a lifelong impression. Following in her father's ethic of writing dedicated to a moral purpose, Stowe wrote for her entire adult life. Her first subject was religion, then New England life (including the Pilgrims), but as her family's focus began to realize that the central American evil was slavery, she used her clout as a writer to reveal that stain. While her brother Henry risked being charged with treason in his hard support for abolitionist insurrectionists, she simply revealed the heinous inhuman truth of men owning humans as chattel, fully supported in American law and the US Supreme Court.

Rather than invoking biblical or even political condemnation, holding a mirror to evil allowed every reader to see or deny his or her own blindness to it. In writing *The Coral Ring* in 1843, Stowe used storytelling to show drunkenness and slavery in terms no sermon could convey.

In 1851, after Stowe moved to Maine, where her husband taught at Bowdoin, she wrote a series of articles for the Washington-based antislavery weekly *National Era*. Originally the series was slated for three or four episodes to "paint a word picture of slavery." Forty installments later, Stowe began to nationally galvanize the outrage that her family, and New England, had felt for generations.

Uncle Tom's Cabin was based on the Stowe and Beecher families' personal experience. In Ohio, the Stowes hired a woman servant from Kentucky. Ohio law allowed the woman to leave her status as a slave while there. But her master came looking for her, so brother Henry Ward Beecher secreted her away to avoid a semi-legal abduction back to slavery.

Harriet Beecher Stowe's Gothic Revival house in Hartford.

The federal Fugitive Slave Law of 1850 settled the legal contradiction of humans being possessions in some states while living free in others. The legitimization of chattel slavery, and Harriet Beecher Stowe's personal witness, compelled her to write the two-volume book that sold three hundred thousand copies in its first year and was ultimately translated into sixty languages.

President Lincoln met her during the Civil War and glibly noted, "So you're the little woman who wrote the book that started this great war."

Many books followed, often with a moral message but increasingly devoted to fiction, until her death at age eighty-five in Hartford.

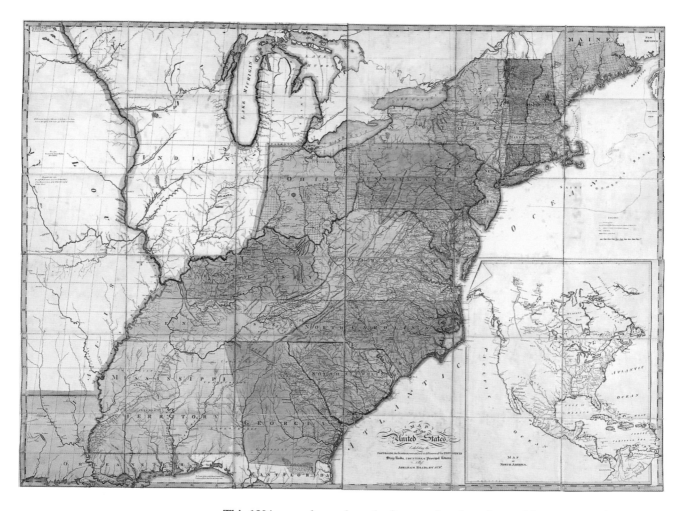

This 1804 map, changed much after two decades, shows eighteen states, the Louisiana Territory, Mississippi Territory, East Florida, Orleans Territory, and Indiana Territory, as well as "Post-Roads, the situations, connexions & distances of the Post-Offices Stage Roads, Counties, & Principal Rivers."

Where We Live Now

7

Religious freedom, local autonomy, abolition, suffrage, and industrialization all played out their cutting-edge realities in New England. In short, the country has come to where New England has led it.

New England came out of World War II changed, but with less change than any other part of America. Factory life had been part of New England life for over a century before World War II transformed entire counties in dozens of other states, coast to coast, with huge military bases, giant industrial facilities, and greatly expanded universities.

Huge investments in naval facilities made parts of coastal New England even more developed and massively productive. Helicopters were a tiny part of the war effort, but airplane production blossomed, and airplane engines made several New England cities and towns proud. The facilities were already there, greatly expanded but, unlike some other parts of America, whole New England towns were not built in 1942 for the war effort.

New England was infused with new energy and capacity, but other parts of America were changed in ways they had not seen since the Civil War ended an entire economy.

Sweeping Changes, Extreme Consequences

Live by infrastructure, and you may die from it. The same railroads that made mid-nineteenth-century New England so efficient and productive exploded that capacity south and west, sowing industrialization far beyond New England. In American infrastructure's second act, the federal highway system completely changed the city/country divide in every state that had cities.

The GI Bill flooded New England's densely arrayed educational system with hundreds of thousands of new students. The newly empowered federal investment in science that created the nuclear option that ended the war was extended to make places like Harvard, Yale, and MIT cutting-edge engines of discovery. The influx of expat professors from war-threatened, then wrecked, Europe transformed the academic climate of the intellectual breadbasket of America into hotbeds of architectural expression, cultural insurgency, and academic argument. New England's WASP inbred intelligentsia received a dose of new blood in a wave of unfiltered and brilliant minds speaking in a variety of accents.

The decade following World War II was perhaps more extreme for New England than any other part of the country. While the Jim Crow South was locked in a segregated society until Ike's second term, millions of African Americans came North in a huge wave of infra-immigration that held up a mirror to the latter-day epicenter of both emancipation and legal equity to reveal a fair amount of prejudice and social stress.

As the death of the New England agriculture ossified into thousands of abandoned farms and second-growth forests, the clear-cutting through

Facing page: Map showing the scope of rail and telegraph lines in the New England states, 1854. By the mid-1850s New Englanders were committed users of the new technology of railroads and telegraphs.

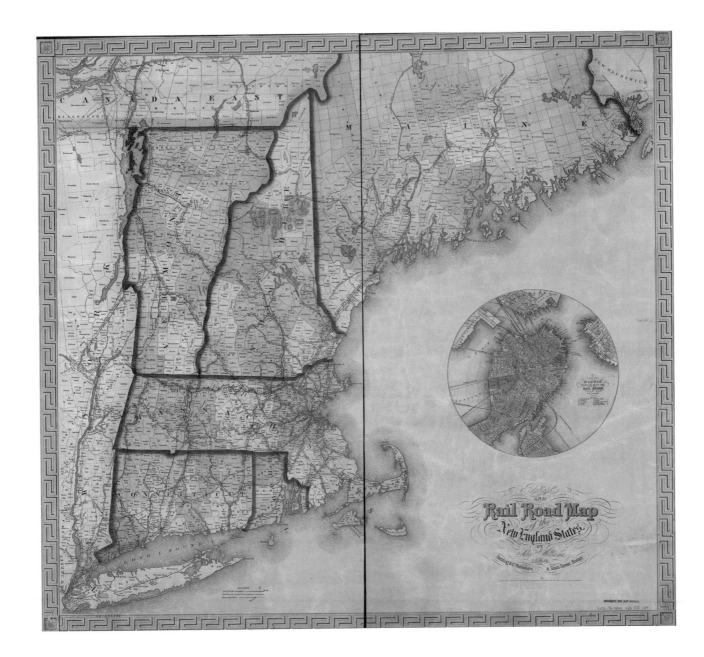

Telegraph AND

Rail Road Map

of the

New England States

BY

Alex. Williams

1854

Redding & Co. Publishers,   8 State Street, Boston

towns and countrysides of the national highway systems took the coastal downtowns of New Haven, Providence, and Boston into split, broken, and wrecked relationships with their harbors—true in other American cities, but without the three-century-context of rended cultural, architectural, and human realities via the blade of automotive expedition.

Where We Live Today

Houses are starting points for every culture. Whether yurts, teahouses, teepees, or castles, all civilizations have places to live.

What makes New England homes distinctive? How would a foreigner know a New England home when she sees it? Like all buildings in all cultures, present-day homes are based on history—a place's cultural database. Identification is easier when the database is large, and as the oldest part of the country, New England certainly has the largest database.

A few centuries ago New England was simply the spawn of runaways, children of a broken home, which was England. Christianity was the religion, and English was the language. But a few centuries of other immigrants running toward freedom and opportunity have been absorbed and helped tilt New England away from its puritanical axis.

But some things have not changed. The difficult weather is among the most variable on the continent, with deep snows, one-hundred-degree days, hurricane-force winds, and sunny/cloudy/rainy variability on an hourly basis. And education is still woven into New England's economic base.

What does that mean about our homes? Not the tract-home commodities that sell over worldwide Zillow feeds like so many hog

Righter Farm Villa. When the architecture of twenty-first-century homes seek to offer New England roots in contemporary design, the crisp detailing and iconic details of Colonial style have fresh application amid the lush landscape.

bellies, but the homes New England architects design in New England, for New Englanders? The renovations are easier to appreciate as they dance with the living past, like the rest of New England.

The new homes designed for new New England are obviously homeowner and site specific and thus can be modernist sculpture or historicist 3-D-printed Xeroxes of what has gone before. But there are some new homes, new takes on what it is to be at home, your home, embedded in New England now—not mimicking California or Santa Fe or 1837. There are contemporary homes that are not contemporary in "style"—nor are they a traditional "style" that might be built in a theme park—but there are homes built in the here and now that embrace New England's unique combination of climate, character, and complexity.

New England's homes deal with weather—in any century: Protection from snow, driving rain, and baking sun means roofs, like those designed by Jeremiah Eck, are built to last, just like those of their great-great-great-grandparents.

Here are some homes and some architects that find inspiration in the culture of New England—right now:

Jeremiah Eck has been designing homes throughout New England for over twenty-five years from his Massachusetts office, Eck McNeely Architects, Inc. Tiny homes, big homes, expensive homes, modest homes, but the aesthetic is always keyed to one starting point: the site.

Having taught at Harvard and written several books, Eck is clear that the site and "the face of home," as he puts it, have to speak in one voice: this is uniquely imperative in New England, where each site's view, aquifer, subsoil, and landscape are as variable as the colors of the autumn leaf explosion.

The shape, exposure, and interior layout of every home respond to the intricacies of these sites: The detailing, materials, and light allusions to a crafty tradition make durability in a rough climate expressively artful.

The interiors are nothing an ascetic Puritan could understand, as they are full of love and care for the occupants' comfort and fondest desires, but the scale is tightly calculated to be both intimate and unified with what the site has to offer.

Jim Righter founded his firm over thirty years ago in Boston, and partners have come on to extend the form's breadth and reach, but there is one distinctive continuity: completeness. It would be easy to leave well enough alone, let a detail or thirty go unexamined, perhaps rely on answers already given on other projects from a huge portfolio.

But easy answers beg interesting questions. And there are no questions that are uninteresting to Albert, Righter & Tittman Architects. The fascination with fine-tuning has a hard-edged basis in fitting the New England context.

Righter Farm Villa. From the rear the covered porch extends along the entire back side of the house so that you can sit outside and enjoy the landscape in any season.

The balance with creativity and fit, between past, present, and future is uniquely found in New England, and these architects delight in the depth of existing context that is addressed in their work in concert with each site and client. Invention without foundation is a monologue. The harmonies found in the grounding of creativity in the deep background of New England history permeate what their homes offer up to their occupants.

The homes of the original settlers of New England had to sustain their occupants, or they would surely die in a completely hostile environment. The homes of twenty-first-century Yankees are only successful if they sustain occupancy as well: While survival is not as threatened now as it was then, the extreme investment of building well makes the sustenance of its occupants critical—or why build anything new in a house-rich environment?

Jim Estes has been at building business for decades, mostly houses—and his firm Estes/Twombly Architects of Newport, Rhode Island, creates homes that are at once cleanly modern and yet completely New England.

Perhaps it's just the reality that shedding snow, keeping the rain out, getting in the shade in the summer, and letting the sun heat in the winter just make the shapes and siting of their homes fit a simple sense of the beauty found in usefulness. But more than stoic repose in the verdant rawness of New England's varied sites, it's the crisp reduction of detail to two criteria: necessary and delightful that make their homes both crisp and rich.

The repeated loving use of contrast between materials is never stilted affect; it simply reflects the right architectural tool for the job of living without unnecessary upkeep.

Swamp Yankees never let go of what might be useful, but also never spent money that was unnecessary: The embrace of utility and enrichment that material distinctions reflect—metal, wood, glass, paint—has a delight not found in a "style."

The ethos of doing more with less, but doing all that is necessary is also the Swamp Yankee way: It's also the Estes/Twombly way.

Why are these homes distinctly of New England? Of course they could be built anywhere—and all of these architects do beautiful work outside of New England. But the homes these architects create are relentlessly creative—just like the soul of New England. Socrates may have said that "the unexamined life is not worth living," but these architects could dovetail that thought in their work product. For all of these gifted designers, and many others in New England, the unexamined house is not worth building.

Jim Estes is an architect from Rhode Island. His work is spontaneously both New England and Modern, simultaneously and inseparably. Embodying the informality of farmhouse with the edge of twenty-first-century line and shape, his creativity relies on history and reaches forward from its baseline into New England landscape.

Seven Exceptional Gables

Captain John Turner was the son of an indentured servant who came from England to the New World in the early days of the Massachusetts Bay Colony. By age twenty-five, when Turner was on his way to extraordinary success as a hat and shoe merchant, he built the best house he could afford, which was a four-bedroom high gentry house, bigger and better than anything in Salem, Massachusetts.

Just like the McMansion zeitgeist of recent history, New England's seventeenth-century high achievers thought "more" was "better," and at his death, only twelve years after he built his home, Turner had acquired five more houses, a few ships, and two hundred acres of land.

In his spare time, he aggressively added onto his home and enriched its detailing with fine finishes and appurtenances. Once his son, John Turner Jr., took ownership of the home, he felt the need to further distinguish the very evolved house and recreated it to the new Georgian style, with still more additions.

John Turner Jr.'s son, John Turner III, went so far as to extend the house to more than seventeen rooms and to a size of 8,000 square feet (including huge cellars) in the 1770s. Just one original exterior wall remained outside in the agglomerated home. But John III squandered the family fortunes and sold the house in 1782 to ship captain Samuel Ingersoll. The Ingersolls were related to legendary New England author Nathaniel Hawthorne by marriage and regularly had him over to play cards. Samuel's daughter, Susanna, remained in the home and eventually became a recluse inside it.

Although he denied the connection in the book's foreword, Hawthorne wrote into his 1851 *The House of the Seven Gables* a central character, Hepzibah Pyncheon, whom many associate with Susannah

Ingersoll. The house was even dubbed "the House of Seven Gables" in
an 1870 town guidebook, when it, by then, had only three remaining
gables.

Susannah's son Horace squandered the family fortune and sold the
house in 1879. Finally the home came to be owned by another serial
renovator, Caroline Emmerton, who wanted to create a museum that
embodied the early twentieth-century desire to define an inherent,
hard-edged, legitimate American culture, one birthed and bathed in
New England colonial culture and later dubbed the Colonial Revival
movement.

Emmerton hired a Boston architect, Joseph Everett Chandler, who
fully bought into a unique colonial culture as expressed in architecture. There followed a three-year renovation, from 1908 to 1910, that

brought the home back to the crazy quilt of its status as an eighteenth-century timber mansion. The renovation expanded the house to include the "cent shop" that Hawthorne's character Hepzibah Pyncheon had, plus a secret stair, insulation, and Georgian paneling.

With classic American bravado, a four-bedroom home had once again morphed into a 9,100-square-foot museum to itself, America, and one of New England's literary lions.

Modern Tolerance

New England has always harbored, and perhaps passively encouraged, the cultural cutting edge. Radical theological refugees found a foothold here. Revolutionaries, abolitionists, and suffragists were born here, too.

So it should not be surprising that the exodus of radical Modernist architects fleeing Hitler's atrocities (and Fascist Neoclassicism) not only found safe harbor and support in New England.

One of these safe harbors was a town in Connecticut that might be considered by definition traditional: New Canaan, a place that venerates the Colonial in its architecture and the WASP in its demographics. About seventy miles away from New Canaan at the venerable Wadsworth Atheneum, the American fine arts–focused museum in Hartford, a quirky new director was appointed in 1927, the model of WASP sophistication. A. Everett "Chick" Austin blew the minds of people in Connecticut who had been lulled into expectations of the institution's steady traditionalism by acquiring Modern work and showing voluble support for the Modern movement in general.

No less than the Modern master architect Charles-Édouard Jeanneret, better known as Le Corbusier, visited Hartford and declared that

Austin was turning the "little town in upper Connecticut into a place where burns the lamp of the mind."

New Canaan Modernist icebreaker Philip Johnson touted that Austin had changed Mark Twain's hometown into "the navel of the world." That high-level encouragement made the sophisticates who had second homes in "the country" follow Johnson and other "starchitects" to New Canaan. The cluster of architects even had a name, the Harvard Five, and included Johnson, Marcel Breuer, Landis Gore, John M. Johansen, and Eliot Noyes—most very successful before their domestic dabbling in Fairfield County, and all teaching at Harvard.

Forty miles east and north of New Canaan is the Yale School of Architecture in New Haven, which brought many of the Euro-Mods to that little New England city as well. The modernization started with the 1953 commission for the Yale University Art Gallery by Louis Kahn, who one-upped himself in 1969 with the Yale Center for British Art across the street. The dam then broke for wildly expressive Modernist expressions by Eero Saarinen, Paul Rudolph, Kevin Roche, and Charles Moore, involving more than one hundred significant Modernist buildings, as conferred by the New Haven Preservation Trust.

Before breaking the Gothic/Colonial/Classical straightjacket at Yale, Harvard brought a big chunk of the Bauhaus School over from Germany in 1937, led by Walter Gropius, the "Pied Piper of Modernism," although Modernist houses had existed in Cambridge since 1932. Mies van der Rohe, Alvar Aalto, and later I. M. Pei and others followed Gropius.

Gropius also created his own firm, The Architect's Collaborative (TAC), and actually defined a style called Cambridge Modern. The firm grew huge, reaching almost four hundred employees soon after Gropius's passing. Of note is that two of the founding "collaborators" were women: Sally Harkness and Jean Fletcher were latter-day architectural suffragettes in the white male world of mid-twentieth-century building design.

There were, of course, miscalculations. Just as the Puritans threw the music out of worship and demanded purity of belief of those they baptized, Modernist architects made buildings in New England that the mainstream of New England simply rejected as too alien. Kevin Roche's New Haven Coliseum was torn down in 2007. Kallmann McKinnell & Knowles's Boston City Hall has become nearly universally reviled. Breuer's Pirelli building now enters its second decade of vacancy in the parking lot of the New Haven Ikea.

Contrast can be alluring, even inspiring. And nowhere else in America could the new find so rich a complementary context than the antiquity of New England, which makes Modernism's case for its devotees.

House—Past, Present, and Future "Colonial" as a Brand

In 1925, about forty years before the historic preservation movement launched in the United States, a Boston architect thought that history could become alive in contemporary homes. This thirty-year-old architect's insight happened thirty years before Walt Disney built history anew in Disneyland—the first place where historic pastiche was aggressively used to create nostalgia.

The architect was Royal Barry Wills, a recent graduate of MIT's architecture school. Wills thought that "Colonial" was not an archaic aesthetic but one that was ardently and actively loved in both symbol

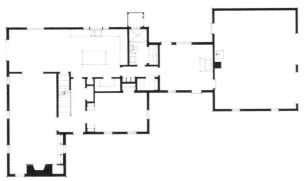

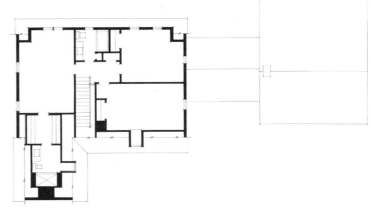

The center hall Colonial may just be the one signature American home that is present in almost every market in the United States. Its New England roots are undeniable, but its flexible evolution beyond its frontal symmetry makes this base plan adaptable to every environment and lifestyle.

Pages 258–60: Architect Royal Barry Wills, his children, and their children have carried on a legacy of Colonial home design that has had unprecedented sustainability over three-quarters of a century: Something about simple lines, uniform detailing, and gentle massing touches the American heart through a New England sensibility.

and substance by millions of families. He believed that the one near universal residential access point for the burgeoning middle-class home ownership (especially in New England) was the Colonial.

The idea that buildings embody history was nothing new, although typically those buildings were associated with a person or event: Presidents' birthplaces, forts, and civic icons all were windows to history because they were physically part of it.

But young architect Royal Barry Wills had a completely different and, as it turns out, abiding idea: that a lot of people want their homes to have all the latest conveniences, but also to feel as comfortable, inside and out, as your favorite pair of blue jeans. "Cutting edge" by definition cuts, and "antique" is a straitjacket of long-gone technologies, values, and lifestyles.

Working for Turner Construction as a draftsman out of college in 1925, Wills was itching to do creative work and so convinced the *Boston Transcript* newspaper to publish his unbuilt designs as a way to boost the paper's builder advertising (and his own baby architectural practice).

Intuitively Wills knew that the most generic of built shapes, a symmetrical, gable-roofed rectangular box with a central chimney was embedded in the American consciousness as "home." Careful cladding and windowscaping made the box a home. That resulting home's characteristics were culturally defined as "Colonial," and that particular Colonial was a Cape Cod.

Unlike the jot-and-tittle detailing imposed on the previous century's style fetishes (Arts & Crafts, Richardson Romanesque, Victorian, Adam, Queen Anne), a Royal Barry Wills Colonial is both relaxed in plan and astringent in material application. Perhaps analogous to Shingle Style on a low-fat diet, the core of a Royal Barry Wills Colonial design allows the landscape on the outside and the furnishings on the inside to express

"Cutting edge" by definition cuts, and "antique" is a straitjacket of long-gone technologies, values, and lifestyles.

Facing page: Few architects have ever made the impression of Royal Barry Wills. He saw through "style" to create Colonial Revival , which made comfort the top priority when America came home in the mid-twentieth century from foreign wars. He was beloved in America but was decidedly New England in his origins and outlooks, and he launched a national career in the popular press.

themselves: Its gentle touch, all clad in white, allows for the expressions of each individual homeowner's tastes and sense of style.

Within a year of publishing his designs, Royal Barry Wills had enough commissions that he could start a thriving home design practice. Wills knew that homes were the single most expensive investment and the one possession that was both intimate and public, so he created a very simple set of descriptive truths of good design that anyone could understand.

Apply these "rules" and include huge central fireplaces, modern kitchens and baths, careful clapboard/shingle spacing, and often opened-up interiors, and voilà, a Royal Barry Wills Colonial. Of course the shapes and names varied: saltbox, center hall, garrison Colonial. But the dead-simple, soft, and comforting palette of materials created homes of various sizes and budgets for the next ninety years—and counting.

It's one thing to be a talented designer, excellent technician, and responsible professional, but Wills also wrote eight books, all but one directed to the homeowner, not to fellow architects. The book titles and drawings are as inviting as the accessible Yankee language he used to write them: *Houses for Good Living, Planning Your Home Wisely*, and *Houses Have Funny Bones*. One of the books published the Modernist designs of then unknown Eliot Noyes, an associate in the firm Royal Barry Wills Associates who became a Modernist maven.

The firm's work was published by *Better Homes and Gardens, House Beautiful, Parade*, and *Country Living*, and has been featured on television in recent years. Throughout his career Wills sought recognition by entering design competitions (two dozen of them); he won a gold medal from President Hoover in 1932 for the National Better Homes Competition.

LIFE

ROYAL BARRY WILLS

BOSTON ARCHITECT DESIGNS THE KINDS OF HOUSES MOST AMERICANS WANT

BLUEPRINT IN HAND, ARCHITECT WILLS SITS IN AN UNFINISHED WINDOW OF ONE OF HIS LATEST HOUSES, BEING BUILT ON ATLANTIC COAST AT NAHANT, MASS.

Scattered about the U.S. are some 1,100 houses which long before the housing shortage were receiving the longing stares of almost everyone who passed them by. They were designed by Royal Barry Wills, a Boston architect whose products seem to be an almost perfect fulfillment of the sentimental American ideal of what a home should be.

Most of Mr. Wills's houses are early American in design—Cape Cod cottages, houses with saltbox roofs or garrison houses with overhanging second stories. Besides designing real houses Wills

has designed several hundred on paper and published them in six books which have a combined sale of 520,000, making him the nation's most popular architectural author.

Solidly entrenched as the leading U.S. designer of small traditional houses, Wills has become a focal point for the distaste of many of the country's more vociferous but less popular modern architects. They call him a copyist and an opportunist and scorn his lack of enthusiasm for designing "machines for living." In rebuttal Wills maintains

that good residential architecture should be primarily emotional and, like good art, be a part of the people and understood by them—a status which modern architecture cannot yet claim.

On the following pages LIFE presents a portfolio of Wills houses in photographs and sketches. Like the modernists Wills tries to build as much practicality into them as he can but insists in the sacrifice of such things as knotty pine panels, exposed hand-hewn beams, eight-foot fireplaces and windows filled with tiny leaded-glass panes.

CONTINUED ON NEXT PAGE

67

Fall College Fashions

AUGUST 26, 1946 **15** CENTS
YEARLY SUBSCRIPTION $5.50

But one Depression-era competition provided spectacular results that took an already successful firm to the height of popular recognition. In 1938 *Life* staged a competition, "Eight Homes for Modern Living," in which four families each reviewed two designs sized and priced to fit their needs. Royal Barry Wills ended up going face-to-face with none other than the first American starchitect—Frank Lloyd Wright. Well, the New England Colonialist beat the Midwestern purveyor of "Usonian" homes (miniaturized Prairie-style houses). Wills's winning

Prickly Mountain
Crazy Kids Flower in the Traditional Freedom of Vermont

In terms of building, it could be said that Vermont may have the most pungently distilled legacy in New England. In the past it had virtually no building code for private homes. The logic was that you had the right to endanger your own life. Freedom as a cultural imperative has a special meaning in New England, as the flash points of the Revolution and its firebrands found support in the region.

In the 1960s, America had its safe post–World War II respite broken by baby boomers demanding the freedom not to be drafted, to love who and when they wished, to wear hair and clothing that defied conventional aesthetics. Naturally the architecture students of the day wanted their buildings to reflect this freedom from traditional rules and expectations.

Yale School of Architecture's Dave Sellers, vowed never to be an ivory tower designer who was clueless about how to actually build what he designed.

In 1964, at the advent of the "why not?!" ethos, Sellers set about to find a place to build. He sought a "natural valley the size of Manhattan" to attract people who could afford to build country homes. Oceanfront property was promising but expensive.

It took a year but he and first one other, then many more developers, found that New England's inability to sustain a viable agricultural economic base offered a fortuitous reality—cheap land. When farmland cannot produce enough food to make a profit, and it's hundreds of miles from urban centers, it simply sells for whatever price the farmer can get.

Sellers and his 1965 cohorts found 425-plus acres of abandoned farm land in the Mad River Valley of north-central Vermont, and, after one of his fellow Ivy League students sat on a raspberry bush, the twentysomething-year-old visionaries declared their venture to be Prickly Mountain.

Prickly Mountain is a place where the Yankee spirit of inspired hard work overcame the realities of money and fear to create dozens of wildly experimental homes in a place where antiques and provenance were the order of the day. Initially, Sellers and his business partners sold lots of land at a thousand dollars apiece. News of this

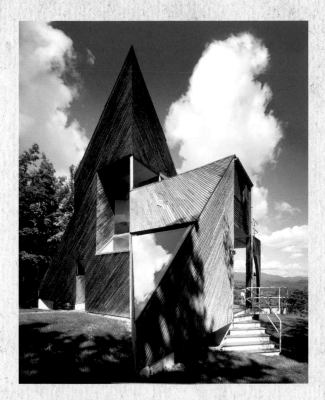

clients, and experimenters in ways no academic studio could ever offer—an "architectural blast-off" according to *P/A*. Houses were designed as they were being built, creating architectural performance art in real time. The young builders/dreamers created genres out of construction alchemy such as "plywood houses," and "wild beam theory." Ultimately the wildly entrepreneurial spirit of Prickly Mountain had spin-offs that are truly profitable: the Vermont Castings Stove Company, Yestermorrow Design/Build School, several innovative energy companies, and any number of relatively successful side developments of commercial properties.

The Sibley/Pyramid House (built 1967) and the Tack House (built 1966) were a result of Sellers and Co.'s design-build process that was more like making art than the standard methods of building homes.

pie-in-the-sky endeavor spread, thanks to media coverage by *LIFE* magazine, the *New York Times*, and an architectural journal, *P/A*, who touted the venture's allure of newness amid the trappings of New England's history.

Workers arrived in bunches, many of them students drawn to a $500 stipend and free food for a summer of hard labor. The so-called establishment was left back at architecture school; at Prickly Mountain the students were the builders, creation on the pages of *Life* magazine was the era's equivalent of a home-design *American Idol*, and it received recognition that made a great career a legendary one.

Over three thousand homes have been built from the designs of the firm in the ninety years, three generations, and more than fifty years after Royal Barry Wills passed on.

The Colonial style as used by Wills was not a replication, or even homage; it is simply the distillation of the carpenterly craft of New England common sense building into a universal solvent of residential design. The authentic need not be original. That just may be the motto of New England.

Place Your Wagers

In an ironic parallel to our reacquired taste, the forgotten native people of New England—the original residents you met at the beginning of this book—have taken the statutory accommodation of the conquerors and, using wisdom born of bitter experience, reanimated their economic viability.

With their ancient status as unsurrendered owners, New England Native Americans created a niche of profitability that accommodates a need for tourist attractions—that is, casinos. Currently, the Mohegan and Mashantucket Pequot tribes each operate gigantic casinos in Connecticut (with a joint casino planned near Hartford), while other tribes operate casinos in Rhode Island, New Hampshire, and Maine. Massachusetts has several more native casinos planned. MGM Springfield opens in late 2018; the Wynn Everett, in Everett, plans to open in June 2019.

Here in the twenty-first century, there are twice as many self-declared Native Americans in New England as there were before World War II. Tribal identities are becoming renewed, not assimilated. The tribes have learned what others have learned about New England: Good ideas with one eye on history find reward with hard work.

The Power of Knowledge

Our culture, not just New England's but America's culture, is inexorably trending to the power of knowledge, information, and the informed use of our minds to maximize our effectiveness, the benefits of freedom, and the natural potential in each person. The twenty-first-century culture of each human's rights to free and meaningful expression in work, belief, and productively has as its incubator, facilitator, and harbor, the places where technology, aesthetics, and intellectual pursuits are given full embrace: the university.

What incubates in many New England cities are places where technology, culture, and commerce connect and thrive. These are places where the mind is nurtured at a time of technological explosion, when the mind is as useful as John Deere's steel plow was to the early nineteenth-century farmer.

New England is the one place where America's fresh intolerance for pretense and its sense of historic truths come together. New England is both "can do" and "what if." It's the place where Eaton and Davenport conspired to manifest their deepest convictions in a city. It's where Eli Whitney saw a problem and fixed it one hundred times. Where farmers not only built walls with the backbreaking waste product of their fields but stuck at farming, knowing they were putting their

In the twenty-first century, there are twice as many self-declared Native Americans in New England as there were before World War II.

The stout pride of New England's own Harvard University is present in this 1744 chapel, renovated first in 1850 and again in 1999. Its brick-rendered temple form has an exquisitely ornamented pediment at its gable roof face, and the dynamic contrast between raw masonry and painted wood serves to complement the desire for history in the New World.

Facing page: Yale is an amazing ensemble of buildings and resulting courtyards. Built in spurts, few of the pre-nineteenth-century buildings remain, but the early twentieth-century flood of collegiate Gothic style, predominately rendered by architect James Gamble Rogers, can be seen here in Harkness Tower (top photo, on right) and the stacks of Sterling Library (bottom photo, upper left).

lives where their values were. Once upon a time, New England was half a globe away from legitimate education, but today it has spawned unparalleled places of intellectual excellence.

More than any other part of the new country, higher education embodied New England's values of cultural expression, technological innovation, and economic growth. Of the new country's nine colleges, New England had four of them. Ten more were founded before 1800, and all grew enormously through the first half of the nineteenth century.

The 1800 census (the new country's second accounting after the 1790 census) shows a nation totaling 5.4 million people that included nearly 900,000 slaves. New England's population totaled 1,233,011,

The Merritt Parkway
Bringing Shoreline Towns Closer Together

In 1934, Connecticut governor Wilbur Cross announced that the state would begin construction on the Merritt Parkway, a scenic parkway intended to relieve traffic congestion on US Route 1, which roamed through all the mostly affluent towns on the shoreline from the New York state line to Stratford, Connecticut, where the Wilbur Cross Parkway now begins.

The interstate highway system, which ripped through towns and often divided one side from another, rightfully is seen as the child of the Merritt, although in most areas the interstate is more of an ugly stepchild.

The Merritt, as it's called in Connecticut, was the first limited-access highway that would wind through the most scenic areas of Fairfield County,

Excavation of the Merritt Parkway's right-of-way cut a huge gash through the coastal New England countryside, though it provided lots of work for a variety of engineering and building trades during the Depression.

Large automobiles find plenty of roomy highway in this 1941 image taken shortly after the Merritt Parkway opened to traffic.

starting at the beginning of New York's Hutchinson River Parkway and ending near the New Haven County line.

What made the Merritt so special in its day was its parklike beauty and isolation. Also, the variety of overpasses it traveled through created a moving slideshow of architecture of the time. During its construction, each individual overpass was one-of-a-kind, and many were concrete works of art. In the years since it opened, however, many newer overpasses failed to adhere to the standard,

and now these ordinary bridges are mingled in with the unique.

Today the Merritt, which was added to the National Register of Historic Places in 1991, courses through some of the most expensive residential real estate in the country, including towns like Greenwich.

This west-looking aerial view of the Merritt Parkway at its Route 8 intersection shows one of the relatively new cloverleaf interchanges that streamlined entrances and exits to "controlled access" highways.

according to the census. That population accounted for 23 percent of the country's citizens (including slaves) and 44 percent of the nation's colleges.

There are more colleges, universities, and places of higher learning in New England than in any other locale in the world. Including the Massachusetts Institute of Technology, Yale, and Harvard, one-third of the world's top ten centers of knowledge lie in less than 0.01 percent of its landmass.

Back to How It Was

New England secularized before the rest of the country did. Many universities stepped away from their religious roots, religious structures become repurposed, and brunch replaced Sunday mass to an extent that made the rest of America appear as pious as New England's first residents.

The excesses of mid-twentieth-century urban renewal, so outrageously applied to New England's small scale and often livable cities, had such heinous consequences to the local populations that wholesale undoing was often initiated. Downtown Providence had its harbor paved over. Boston had its downtown-crushing Interstate 93 relocated in a twenty-year burial that turned a tone-deaf and brain-dead imposition into an excruciating rectification now known as the Big Dig. New Haven had an entire neighborhood vaporized to create a path for a highway that was never built and that needed $60 million to heal in the twenty-first century by filling in the deep-cut highway and reconnecting the old street grid.

Amid the good intentions of the best and brightest to reinvent New England's cities in the top-down urban design hegemony, suburban residential development kept taking over abandoned farmland. These were followed by malls, and all coalesced into many small villages of bedroom communities. The pre-2008 economic crash came with a wave of McMansion exurb building. This land-gorging sprawl was national in nature, but its impact in the history-infused landscape of New England was particularly misfit.

In the wake of these waves of post–federal highway–facilitated development, most New England towns and villages began to look better and better by comparison. The town green, once the universal spatial solvent of a community's needs, has become a venerated repository of memory. The meetinghouse, once the hybrid manifestation of the joint purpose of God and man, has transitioned from the nobly functional to the iconically reverential.

These one-way transitions from eighteenth-century realities to twenty-first-century cultural embodiments of memory are a straight-line manifestation of cultural evolution. There is a different pattern of New England evolution, where ancient truths become reaffirmed in new realities. These changes are not undoing huge errors, like building a superhighway wall between historic city centers and the sea, but this path reaffirms human desires that only history can validate.

However, every site within every New England city has a history: settlement, improvement, and, lately, abandonment and some spotty reclamation. The retrospective revisionism of this generation's conventional wisdom is that "sustainability" is the only moral, ethical, and smart choice for living.

What does *sustainable* mean? The buzz words are *density* (more people in less space), *diversity* (live/work/learn/play together, not distinct) and *walkability* (implying that a car is not a necessity). New England encompasses the towns that existed between 1620 and 1950. "New"

Downtown Portland, Maine

zoning replicates the commonsense Swamp Yankee truths of not wasting a thing, not passing up a chance to spend now to avoid spending more later.

What is old is new again. The walkable downtowns of Portland, New Haven, and Cambridge are now chic and hip. The "sustainable" hipster heaven of "walkable downtown living" is anything but new—it's the legacy of 350 years of human experience.

Appendix A: Native American Place Names Across New England

Connecticut

Aspetuck River (and town): (Paugussett) "at the high place"

Cockenoe Island: (Montauk) from the name of a seventeenth-century native interpreter

Coginchaug River: (Wangunk) "place where fish are dried/cured"

Congamond Lake (on Massachusetts border): (Nipmuck) "long fishing place"

Connecticut: (Mohegan) from Quinnehtukqut, "long river place" or "beside the long tidal river"

Cos Cob: (Mohegan) from cassacubque, "high rocks"

Hammonassett Point: (Hammonassett) "place of sand bars"

Hockanum River (and community): (Podunk) "hook"

Housatonic River: (Mahican) "beyond the mountain"

Mashantucket: (Pequot) "to the west" or "western"

Mashapaug Pond: (Nipmuck) "large pond"

Massapeag: (Mohegan) "place at the large cove"

Mohawk Mountain: (eastern Iroquois tribe) Algonquian term for their western enemies; "wolves," "hungry animals," or "cannibals"

Mohegan: (tribe) "hungry animal" or "wolf"

Moodus River (also reservoir and village): (Wangunk) from *mache moodus* or "bad noises," also called "the Moodus noises." A variety of sources claim that areas around the river still emit strange noises. In 2011, seismologists explained that small earthquakes create the sounds, according to a news account in the *Hartford Courant*.

Moosup: (Narragansett) from a chief named Mausup

Mystic River (and town): (Pequot/Mohegan) "great tidal river"

Naugatuck River (and town): (Quinnipiac) "single tree"

Natchaug River: (Nipmuck) "between rivers"

Nepaug Reservoir: (Wangunk) "fresh pond"

Niantic River (and town): (Nehantic) "point of land on tidal river" or "of long-necked waters"

Norwalk River (and city): (Algonquian) *noyank* or "point of land"

Oronoque: (Quinnipiac) "curved place" or "land at the bend"

Pachaug River (and pond): (Narragansett) "at the turning place"

Pataguanset Lake: (Niantic) "at the round, shallow place"

Pawcatuck River (Rhode Island border): (Niantic/Pequot) "the clear divided (tidal) stream"

Pequabuck: (Wangunk) "clear, open pond"

Pistapaug Pond: (Quinnipiac) "muddy pond"

Pocotopaug Lake: (Wangunk) "divided pond" or "two ponds"

Poquetanuck: (Mohegan) "land broken up" (like dried mud cracking)

Poquonock River (and bridge): (Algonquian) "cleared land"

Quaddick Reservoir: (Nipmuck) "bend in river" or (Narragansett) "boggy place"

Lake Quassapaug: (Quinnipiac) "big pond" or "big rock"

Quinebaug River (and town): (Nipmuck) "long pond"

Quinnipiac River: (Quinnipiac) "where we change our route"

Lake Quonnipaug: (Quinnipiac) "long pond"

Lake Waramaug: (Mahican) "good fishing-place"

Saugatuck River: (Paugussett) "outlet of the tidal river"

Scitico: (Nipmuck) "land at the river branch"

Shenipsit Lake: (Mohegan) "at the great pool"

Shepaug River: (Tunxis) "great pond"

Shetucket River: (Mohegan) "land between rivers"

Shunock River: (Mohegan) "stony place" or possibly "place between streams"

Skungamug River: (Nipmuck) "eel-fishing place"

Taconic: (Mahican) "steep ascent"

Wangum Lake: (Paugussett) "bend/crooked"

Wangumbaug Lake: (Nipmuck) "crooked pond"

Willimantic River (and town): (Mohegan/Nipmuck) "good cedar swamp"

Winnepauk: (Mahican) "beautiful pond"

Wononpacook Pond: (Mahican) "land at the bend in the pond"

Wononskopomuc Lake: (Mahican) "rocks at the bend in the lake"

Wopowaug River: (Wangunk) "crossing place"

Wyassup Lake: (Mohegan) "flags" or "rushes"

Yantic River (and town): (Mohegan) "as far as the tide goes up this side of the river"

Maine

Amitgon pontook: (Abenaki) "place at the falls where fish are dried/cured"—Lewiston Falls

Androscoggin River: (Abenaki) "place where fish are dried/cured"

Aroostook River: (Micmac) "beautiful river"

Aziscohos Lake: (Abenaki) "small pine trees"

caribou: (Abenaki) *kalibu*, "shoveler" (gets food by pawing or shoveling)

Casco Bay: (Micmac) "muddy"

Chebeague Island: (Abenaki) "separated place"

Chemquasabamticook Lake: (Abenaki) "where there is a large lake and rocks"

Chesuncook Lake: (Abenaki) "at the principal outlet"

Chiputneticook Lakes: (Abenaki) "at the place of the big hill stream"

Cobbosseecontee Lake: (Abenaki) "many sturgeon"

Cobscook Bay: (Maliseet) "rocks under water"

Damariscotta (and lake and river): (Abenaki) "many alewives"

Katahdin: (Abenaki) "the principal mountain"

Kennebago Lake: (Abenaki) "long/large pond/lake"

Kennebec River: (Abenaki) "long quiet water"

Kennebunk (and river): (Abenaki) "long sand bar"

Machegony: (Micmac) "shaped like a large knee"—Portland

Madawaska River: (Micmac) "where one river joins another"

Matagamon: (Abenaki) "far on the other side"

Matinicus Island: (Abenaki) "far-out island"

Mattamiscontis Lake: (Abenaki) "many alewives"

Mattawamkeag River (and town): (Abenaki) "fishing beyond gravel bar" or (Micmac) "on a sand bar"

Metinic Island: (Abenaki) "far-out island"

Millinocket (and lake): (Abenaki) "this place is admirable"

Molunkus Pond (and stream): (Abenaki) "ravine"

Monhegan Island: (Micmac/Maliseet) "out-to-sea island"

Mooselookmeguntic Lake: (Abenaki) "moose feeding place"

Muscongus Bay: (Abenaki) "many/large rock ledges"

Musquacook River (and lake): (Abenaki) "muskrat place"

Musquash Lake: (Abenaki) "muskrat"

Nahmakanta Lake: (Abenaki) "many fish"

Nollesemic (and lake): (Abenaki) "resting place at the falls"

Ogunquit: (Micmac) "lagoons within dunes"

Oquossoc: (Abenaki) "place of trout" (a certain trout)

Orono: (Abenaki) from a Chief Joseph Orono

Ossipee River: (Abenaki) "beyond the water"

Passadumkeag: (Abenaki) "rapids over gravel beds"

Passamaquoddy Bay: tribal name; "place of abundance
of pollack"

Pemadumcook Lake: (Maliseet) "extended sandbar place"

Pemaquid: (Micmac) "extended land" (peninsula)

Penobscot River: (Penobscot) "place of descending rocks/ledges"

Piscataqua River (New Hampshire border): (Pennacook) "the place
where the river divides"

Piscataquis River (Abenaki): "at the river branch"

Quoddy Head (Passamaquoddy): abbreviation of "pollack"

Saco (and river): (Abenaki) "flowing out" or "outlet"

Sebago Lake (and town): (Abenaki) "big lake"

Sebasticook Lake: (Penobscot/Abenaki) "almost-through place"

Seboomook Lake (and town): (Abenaki) "at the large stream"

Skowhegan (town): (Abenaki) "watching place (for fish)"

Squapan Lake (and town): (Abenaki) "bear's den"

Umcolcus Lake: (Abenaki) "whistling duck"

Usuntabunt Lake: (Abenaki) "wet head" or possibly "three heads"

Webhannet River: (Abenaki) "at the clear stream"

Massachusetts

Achastapac: (Pocumtuck) "Land of rivers and mountains"

Acoaxet: (Narragansett) "at the fishing promontory" or "place of small pines"

Acushnet River (and town): (Narragansett) "at the cove"

Agawam: (Nipmuck/Pennacook) "low land" (with water) or "place to unload canoes" (possible portage spot)

Annisquam (and river)

Assabet River: (Nipmuck) "at the boggy place"

Assawompset Pond: (Narragansett) "trading place"; (Wampanoag) "place of large upright rock"

Assinippi: (Wampanoag) "rocks in water"

Assonet River (also Cedar Swamp and village): (Narragansett) "at the rock" (the rock in question being Dighton Rock)

Cataumet: (Wampanoag) "at the ocean" or "landing place"

Chappaquiddick Island: (Wampanoag) "separated island"

Chaubunagungamaug, Lake: (Nipmuck/Mohegan) "boundary fishing place"

Chicopee (also falls and river): (Nipmuck) "violent water"

Cochituate: (Natick) "place of swift water"

Cohannet: (Wampanoag or Narragansett) "at the long or pine place"—Taunton

Cohasset: (Natick) "long rocky place"

Congamond Lake: (Nipmuck) "long fishing place"

Cotuit: (Wampanoag) "long planting field"

Cummaquid: (Wampanoag) "harbor"

Cuttyhunk: (Wampanoag) "thing that lies out in the sea"

Hockanum: (Podunk) "hook"

Hockomock Swamp: (Natick/Abenaki) "evil spirit" or "hellish place"; (Narragansett) "hook-shaped place"

Hoosac Tunnel: (Mahican) "rock place"

Humarock: (Wampanoag) "shell place" or "rock carving"

Hyannis: (Wampanoag) name of a seventeenth-century chief, Iyanogh, a local sachem.

Jamaica Plain (and pond): (Natick) "beaver"

Lake Monomonac (New Hampshire border): (Abenaki) "at the very deep place"

Manhan River: (Nipmuck) "island"

Manomet (and point): (Wampanoag) "portage place"

Mashpee: (Wampamoag) "place near great cove"

Massachusetts: (Natick) "by the great hills"—the Blue Hills, south of Boston

Mattapan: (Natick) "resting place" or "end of portage"

Mattapoisett: (Wampanoag) "resting place" or "edge of cove"

Merrimac: (Pennacook) "deep place"

Merrimack River: (Abenaki) "at the deep place"

Minnechaug (regional high school): (Algonquian) "land of berries"

Mishaum Point: (Narragansett) "great neck" or "canoe-landing place"

Monatiquot River: (Massachusetts) "a lookout place"

Monomoy Island (and point): (Wampanoag) "lookout place" or "deep water"

Muskeget Island (and channel): (Wampanoag) "grassy place"

Mystic River: (Natick) "great tidal stream"

Nabnasset: (Nipmuck)

Nahant: (Natick) "the point" or "almost an island"

Nantasket Beach: (Natick/Wampanoag) "at the strait" or "low-tide place"

Nantucket Island: (Wampanoag) "in the midst of waters"; (Narragansett) "far off" or "among the waves"

Nashawena Island: (Wampanoag) "between"

Natick: (tribe) "the place I seek" or "home," "place," "clearing"

Nemasket River: (Wampanoag) "place where the fish are"

Neponset River: (Natick) possibly "a good fall" (easy for canoe travel)

Nonamesset Island: (Wampanoag)

Nonquitt: (Narragansett) "dry or landing place"

Onota Lake: (Mahican) "blue/deep"

Pocasset: (Natick) "where the stream widens"

Pontoosuc: (Mahican/Nipmuck) "falls on the brook"

Poughkeeste: (Wampanoag) "bay with coves"—Buzzards Bay

Quabbin Reservoir: (Nipmuck) "crooked streams"

Quaboag River: (Nipmuck) "before the pond" or abbreviation of "red pond" (m'squ'boag)

Quinebaug River: (Nipmuck) "long pond"

Quinsigamond, Lake: (Nipmuck) "pickerel-fishing place"

Quissett: (Nipmuck) "at the place of small pines"

Sagamore: (Wampanoag) "chief"

Santuit: (Wampanoag) "cool water place"

Saugus: (Natick) "outlet"

Scituate: (Wampanoag) "at the cold spring or brook"

Seekonk: (Narragansett) "wild black goose"; (Wampanoag) "mouth of stream" or "wild goose"

Segreganset River: (Narragansett) "place of hard rocks"

Shawmut Peninsula: (Algonquian) "ferry" or "place to draw up canoes"

Siasconset: (Narragansett) "at the place of many/great bones"

Snipatuit Pond: (Wampanoag) "at the rocky river"

Squibnocket Point (and pond): (Wampanoag) "at the place of dark rocks" (or clay cliff)

Swampscott: (Natick) "place of red rocks"

Taconic Mountains: (Natick) "steep ascent"

Tantiusques: (Nipmuck) "black stuff between the hills"

Tuckernuck Island: (Wampanoag) "round loaf of bread"

Wachusett, Mount (and reservoir): (Natick) "near the mountain"

Waquoit: (Wampanoag) "at the end"

Weweantic River: (Wampanoag) "crooked" or "wandering stream"

New Hampshire

Common languages: Abenaki, Nipmuck, Pennacook

Ammonoosuc River (Upper and Lower): (Abenaki) "small, narrow fishing place"

Amoskeag: (Pennacook) "fishing place"—Manchester

Ashuelot River (and pond): (Pennacook/Natick) "place between"

Canobie Lake: (Abenaki) "abundant water"

Contoocook (and river and lake): (Pennacook) "place of the river near pines"; (Abenaki) "nut trees river"; (Natick) "small plantation at the river"

Coös: (Pennacook) "pine tree"

Hooksett: (Pennacook) possible abbreviation of Annahooksett, "place of beautiful trees"

Mascoma River (and lake): (Abenaki) "much grass," "salmon fishing," or "red rocks"

Massabesic Lake: (Abenaki) "near the great brook"

Nashua River (and city): (Pennacook/Nipmuck) "between streams"

Ossipee River (and town and lake): (Abenaki) "beyond the water"

Paugus Bay: (Abenaki) "small pond"

Pawtuckaway Lake (and mountains): (Abenaki) "falls in the river" or "clear, shallow river"

Pemigewasset River: (Abenaki) "extensive rapids"

Pennacook (village): (tribe) "at the foothills"

Piscataqua River (Maine border): (Pennacook) "place where the river divides"

Piscataquog River: (Abenaki) "place where the river divides"

Souhegan River: (Pennacook/Nipmuck) "watching place"

Squam Lake (and river): (Abenaki) "salmon"

Sunapee, Lake (and town): (Pennacook) "rocks in the water," "rocky pond"

Suncook River (also lakes and village): (Pennacook) "rocky place"

Umbagog Lake: (Abenaki) "clear lake"

Winnipesaukee, Lake (and river): (Pennacook) "land around the lakes" or "good land around lake at mountains"

Winnisquam Lake: (Abenaki) "salmon-fishing place"

Rhode Island

Common languages: (northern) Natick, Nipmuck; (southern) Narragansett

Apponaug: (Narragansett) "where oysters/shellfish are roasted"
or "waiting place"

Canonchet: a seventeenth-century Narragansett chief

Chepachet: (Narragansett) "boundary/separation place"

Conanicut Island: (Narragansett) named for a seventeenth-century
chief, Canonicus

Mount Hope: (from Narragansett *montop* or *montaup*) "lookout place"
or "well-fortified island"

Narragansett Bay (and town): (tribe) "at the narrow point"

Natick: (tribe) "the place I seek" or "home"

Pascoag (and river): (Nipmuck) "the dividing place" (of a river)

Pawtucket: (Narragansett) "at the falls in the river" (i.e., tidal stream)

Pettaquamscutt Rock (and river): (Narragansett) "at the round rock"

Quonochontaug: (Narragansett) "home of the blackfish"

Sakonnet Point: (Narragansett) "home of the black goose"

Scituate Reservoir: (Wampanoag) "at the cold spring/brook"

Shawomet: (Narragansett) "at the peninsula/neck" (i.e., canoe-
landing place)

Usquepaugh: (Narragansett) "at the end of the pond"

Weekapaug: (Narragansett) "at the end of the pond"

Woonsocket: (Nipmuck) "place of steep descent"

Wyoming: (Delaware) "large prairie"

Former names:

Aquidnic: (Narragansett) "the island"—Rhode Island

Manisses: (Narragansett) "little god"; (Niantic) "little island"—Block
Island

Mattoonuc Neck: (Niantic) "place at look-out hill"—Point Judith

Maushapogue: (Narragansett) "land at the great cove"—Cranston

Niwosaket: (Narragansett) "place of two brooks"—Woonsocket

Vermont

Common languages: Abenaki, Mahican

Ascutney, Mount (and village): (Abenaki) "at the end of the river fork"

Bomoseen, Lake (and town): (Abenaki) "keeper of ceremonial fire"

Hoosac Mountains: (Mahican) "stone place"

Jamaica: (Natick) "beaver"

Memphremagog, Lake: (Abenaki) "where there is great expanse of water"

Mozodepo: (Abenaki) "moose-head mountain"—Mount Mansfield

Nickwaket Mountain: (Abenaki) "at the fork" or "home of squirrels"

Nulhegan River: (Abenaki) "log trap" or "deadfall"

Ompompanoosuc River: (Abenaki) "mushy/quaky land"

Ottauquechee River: (uncertain, Natick?) "swift mountain stream"

Passumpsic River (and village): (Abenaki) "flowing over clear, sandy bottom"

Pico Peak: (possibly Abenaki) "the pass/opening"

Pompanoosuc: abbreviation of Ompompanoosuc

Quechee: abbreviation of Ottauquechee

Queneska Island: (Abenaki) "elbow" or "long joint"

Winooski River (and city): (Abenaki) "wild onions."

"Listing Place Names That Bear the Indian Mark" courtesy of Wikipedia, The Free Encyclopedia, s.v. "List of Place Names in New England of Aboriginal Origin," (accessed December 2015), https://en.wikipedia.org/wiki/List_of_place_names_in_New_England_of_aboriginal_origin.

Appendix B:
The Tribes of
New England Today

Abenaki Tribe

The Abenaki are from N'dakinna, a word that means "our homeland," and live in the north of New England and into Canada. The Abenakis are related to the Wabanakis, which encompass the Micmacs and Penobscots. The Abenakis in northern New England include bands that remain in their historical locales around the Connecticut River, in Quebec, and along Lake Champlain. According to the tribe's website (abenakitribe.org), N'dakinna "is nestled among the lakes, rivers, and forests of Vermont's Northeast Kingdom. Our connection to this land cannot be described in any language. It is our birthright and obligation to advocate for our ancestral territory so that its uniqueness and beauty will be protected for the generations to come."

Eastern Pequot Nation

This southeastern Connecticut tribe is currently recognized by the state with a reservation in North Stonington. According to its website (easternpequottribalnation.com), the Eastern Pequot tribe "arose from the ashes" of a 1637 massacre in Mystic, Connecticut, at its Pequot village on Long Island Sound. As many as seven hundred Pequot men, women, and children were burned alive or butchered by the British.

Before the English came, there had been about twenty-six villages on the Connecticut, Pequot, Mystic, and Pawcatuck Rivers, and on coastal islands. According to the website, "The maps of early explorers deemed the Pequot land 'Paradise' because of the abundance of deer, beaver, bear, fox, otter, duck, goose, rabbit, and seal as well as the abundance of edible crops like corn, beans, squash, strawberries, and grapes that were cultivated by the native people; the wild native trees and plants were natural and precious resources that could be exploited for the European markets and for the survival needs of the colonists."

The tribe also was well known for its creation of wampum of purple or white beads made from shells, as well as their elaborate beadwork. "Wampum played a very significant part in the spiritual, cultural, and political lives of the Pequot," according to the tribe's website. "It had a tremendous value as a trading commodity to the Europeans, who would trade whatever wampum they could get their hands on for furs or other marketable commodities which would result in tremendous profits to the Europeans."

After the massacre, the Pequot survivors made it to coastal islands, where they got protection from Wequashcuk and Eastern Nehantic tribes.

After moving from place to place in Connecticut and Rhode Island, the tribe settled in North Stonington, Connecticut, in an area set aside by the colonial authorities for their use., The Eastern Pequot nation says on its website: "Several hundred and possibly more than a thousand acres adjacent to Long Pond and Lantern Hill, a traditional gathering place of the Pequots, and where the Narragansett and Pequot trails formerly intersected, became known as the Eastern Pequot reservation."

According to the tribe, their reservation "has been continually occupied by the Eastern Pequot Tribe since [the] 1670s. A formal deed of the reservation for use of the tribal leader and his followers and descendants was executed and filed in 1683."

Golden Hill Paugussett Indian Tribe

The Golden Hill Paugussett is a state-recognized tribe in Colchester, Connecticut, and one of the oldest and smallest reservations in the United States. Although recognized in 1659, today the reservation is located on just a quarter acre, which only has room for the current chief, Aurelius Piper, and his family. Back before the reservation was recognized by Connecticut, the court decided that it was alright for colonists to take the land, a chunk of which became what is today Bridgeport. In return the tribe received eighty acres, which was also later taken. That left the tribe with the quarter acre where the chief lives. Today, that area comprises the entire tribe of the Golden Hill Paugussetts.

Maliseet Tribe

The tribe is recognized by the Bureau of Indian Affairs (BIA) as the Houlton Band of Maliseet. The tribe's reservation straddles Interstate 95 and is bordered on its eastern side by Canada and the Meduxnekeag River in Maine's Aroostook County. The Maliseets have traditionally occupied areas of the Saint John River Valley. With the 1794 Jay Treaty, Great Britain and the United States set their common boundary here, and the Maliseets were given the right to freely cross the border. Their language belonged to the Algonquin family.

Mashantucket Pequot Nation

The Mashantucket Pequot Nation of southeastern Connecticut resides on one of the oldest continuously occupied Indian reservations in America. The tribe owns Foxwoods Resort Casino, one of the largest in the world, as well as Lake of Isles Golf Course and the MGM Grand at Foxwoods.

According to its website, the tribe is the highest taxpayer and largest employer in Connecticut. Its tribal symbol is a fox, "which stands as a vigilant reminder of the turbulent times they went through when Europeans first arrived in the early seventeenth century." (https://www.mptn-nsn.gov/default.aspx)

The tribe says that it was the "first Native American group within United States to suffer an attempted genocide by Puritan colonists in 1637 (the Pequot War)." In addition to its gambling and resort facilities, the Mashantucket Pequot Nation owns and runs the 85,000-square-foot

Mashantucket Pequot Museum and Research Center in Mashantucket, Connecticut.

Aroostook Band of Micmacs

The Aroostook Band of Micmacs live in Aristook County in northern Maine. The Micmac Nation today is composed of seven districts with twenty-nine bands and a population of approximately thirty thousand.

The Micmac language is an Algonquin one, related to that of the Micmacs' southern neighbors, the Maliseets, Passamaquoddys, Penobscots, and Abenakis. The tribe's website says that "all these northeastern tribes are culturally and linguistically related. Collectively, this group is called the Wabanaki, which means 'People of the Daybreak,' or 'Dawn Land People.'"

Today the Micmacs continue to produce a variety of traditional baskets made of split ash wood, birch bark, and split cedar. The Micmacs are recognized as excellent producers of porcupine quill on birch bark boxes and wooden flowers from strips of maple, cedar, and white birch.

Mohegan Tribe

The Mohegan tribe in southwestern Connecticut has been a functioning and independent entity for centuries. Today the Mohegans (known by most for their casino, Mohegan Sun), though subject to the laws of the state and federal governments, maintain jurisdiction over their land, as well as having their own constitution.

The Mohegans elect a tribal council of nine members and a seven-member council of elders.

The Mohegans gained federal recognition in 1994 and received land in settlement under the Mohegan Nation Land Claim Settlement Act of 1994. The tribe's reservation now resides on a cleaned-up United Nuclear site.

Two years after federal recognition, the tribe opened the Mohegan Sun casino, and it pays 25 percent of its slot-machine revenue to the state. Aside from the federal government, Connecticut's Native American tribes have become the largest source of revenue for Connecticut.

Narragansett Tribe

After sending a fifteen-volume petition to the Bureau of Indian Affairs in 1979, the Narragansett tribe from Rhode Island was federally recognized in 1983 based on an 1880 treaty. According to its website, "State legislation, which transferred title to the Tribe, was enacted in 1985. The Tribe then initiated procedures in 1985 to obtain federal trust status for the settlement land. The land was placed in provisional trust, subject to a completed, tribally approved cadastral survey to determine legal boundaries."

Traditionally the tribe spoke the Narragansett language, an Algonquian language family . The language became almost entirely extinct during the Narragansetts' centuries of living within the larger English-majority society.

Using early twentieth-century texts, the Narragansetts are now trying to revive their native tongue. In the seventeenth century, Roger

Williams documented the Narragansetts' language in *A Key into the Language of America*, which he wrote after learning their language.

The English spoken today in the United States has adopted a number of Native American words and terms, such as *woodchuck*, *squash*, *chocolate*, *caucus*, *toboggan*, *opossum*, and *moose*, in addition to many others.

Nipmuc Nation

According to the University of Massachusetts Boston, "The Nipmuc Indians are the tribal group occupying the central part of Massachusetts, northeastern Connecticut, and northwestern Rhode Island. The Nipmuc Nation is not a federally recognized tribe but a state-recognized band with currently about 500 members based at the Hassanamisco Reservation in Grafton, Massachusetts. This small three-acre reservation is the only parcel of Nipmuc land never to have changed hands; its occupation by Nipmuc people dates back to before contact and colonization. The Nipmuc Indians of Massachusetts have several bands today, including the Chaubunagungamaug of Webster and [the] Natick Nipmuc of Natick, in addition to the Nipmuc Nation."

Penobscot Nation

The Penobscot tribe is one of the four northeastern woodlands tribes of the Wabanaki Confederacy. It maintains a reservation near Bangor, Maine, at Indian Island. Contact with Europeans was not uncommon during the sixteenth century because the fur trade was lucrative and the Penobscot were willing to trade pelts for European goods such as metal axes, guns, and copper or iron cookware. European traders also introduced alcohol to Penobscot communities for the first time.

As happened so often, the Penobscots, who had no immunity to European diseases, suffered greatly from now common childhood diseases such as measles, which killed many of the tribe. Smallpox also took its toll among the tribe.

The Penobscots allied with the French during the French and Indian War and later sided with colonists against the British during the American Revolution. However, in the early years of the nation, when Maine was still part of Massachusetts, the Penobscots ceded most of its land to the state. In the 1970s they sued, citing the state's violation of the 1790 Nonintercourse Act that required congressional approval for the transfer of land from a tribe to a state, which Maine had not done. The tribe's 1981 settlement resulted in an $81.5 million payment, which the Penobscots have used to acquire islands in the Penobscot River as well as several hundred thousand acres across the state.

Schaghticoke Tribal Nation

According to the tribe's website, the Schaghticoke Tribal Nation has been recognized first by the colony of Connecticut and then the state of Connecticut as a separate and distinct tribal entity. Today, the tribe has approximately three hundred members at its reservation in Kent, Connecticut.

The tribe filed for federal recognition in 1994; in January 2004 the Bureau of Indian Affairs granted them federal recognition status but rescinded it on Columbus Day in 2005.

The Mashpee Wampanoag and the Wanpanoag Tribe of Gay Head

The two Wampanoag tribes in Massachusetts each received federal recognition at different times: the Gay Head tribe in 1987 and the Mashpee Wampanoag tribe in 2007. The Gay Head tribe is located on Martha's Vineyard, and the Mashpees are on Cape Cod.

Other Wampanoag groups include the Assonet Band, Herring Pond, Seaconke, and Pocasset.

Index

(Note: Page numbers in *italics* indicate photographs or art.)

United States Children's Bureau, 185
USS *Chesapeake*, 141

van der Rohe, Mies, 257
Vaux, Calvert, 240
Veare, Edward, 33
Vermont
    Billings Farm & Museum, 183
    Prickly Mountain homes, 264–65
Victorian Cottage Residences (Downing), 91
Vikings, 4–5, 8

Wade, L., 28
Wadsworth, William, 214
Wadsworth Atheneum, 256
Ward, John Quincy Adams, 220
Ward, Prof. Henry A., *191*
Ward, Sam, 229
War of 1812, 137, 140–42, 169
Watts Sherman House, 95, 97
Webster, Daniel, 201
Webster, Noah, 122–23, 150
West, Nathaniel, 87

Wheelock, Eleazar, 66
Whitfield, Rev. Henry, 52–53
Whitman, Walt, 194
Whitney, Eli, 150, 168, 169, 267
William Low House, 104
Williams, Roger, 26–27
Williams, W. L., 28
Wills, Royal Barry, 258, 260, 261–63, 266
Winchester, Oliver, 169
Winslow, Edward, 16
Winthrop, Deane, 69
Winthrop, John, 27
Wright, Frank Lloyd, 104, 263

Yale, Elihu, 48–49
    See also Yale University
Yale-Duryea Mills, 149
Yale University, 172, 246, *268*, 269, 272
    School of Architecture, 257

Zobel, Melissa Tantaquidgeon, 2, 15, 18
    on Uncas, 21
    on waterways, 22–23

Acknowledgments

Every book is just the tip of a work iceberg frozen into place by many devoted people. But the authors get their name on the cover—others do not, but were crucial in the book's creation. There would be no book without those who worked so hard to make it happen. First, publisher Jim Childs had faith in the idea that New England had a POV that could be communicated in print and supported our idea. Then Amy Lyons, our editor, saw through the unending words and art to put the book together. But *A Home Called New England* had other essential help, found in intern Will Bogardus, who devotedly went at hundreds of sources to find most of the art you see here—and then followed through on endless loose ends, as did Karen Erickson who served as the authors' administrative assistant.   —*Duo Dickinson*

We would like to acknowledge the Historic American Building Survey, or HABS, which describes itself as "the nation's first federal preservation program, begun in 1933 to document America's architectural heritage," and whose photography database online is deep, wide, and remarkable. We also thank Melissa Tantaquidgeon Zobel Fawcett of the Mohegan Tribe for providing native tribal history over the centuries as the English relentlessly moved to take over tribal land. We appreciate the help and guidance of Dr. Lucianne Lavin, Director of Research & Collections at the Institute for American Indian Studies in Washington, Connecticut. We also thank our editor, Amy Lynn Lyons of Globe Pequot, for her relentless patient prodding, without which two otherwise busy people writing a book together might not have gotten it done.

—*Steve Culpepper*

About the Authors

Duo Dickinson (www.duodickinson.com), based in Madison, Connecticut, is a noted architect with more than 30 years of professional practice, he has built over 700 projects in over 10 states, with budgets ranging from $5,000 to $5,000,000. He is recognized as a maverick within the profession. He is the author of seven books on residential design.

Steve Culpepper hails from redneck northwest Louisiana and graduated from LSU, where he studied English and history, and interned at LSU Press the same year that it published *A Confederacy of Dunces*, which won the Pulitzer Prize and for which he can take no credit. He has worked in all forms of print publishing in his long career. A former newspaper reporter and editor, Culpepper later worked in magazine and book publishing at The Taunton Press as well as in book publishing at Globe Pequot Press, where he was editorial director. After a subsequent stint of freelance writing and editing, Culpepper now enjoys his role as senior editor at *Guideposts*, where he helps oversee the book publishing program for the nationwide faith-based organization founded by Norman Vincent Peale. When he's not squinting at words on a screen he can be found either on a bicycle or hard at work on one of his many unending remodeling and home-improvement projects while staying closely supervised by his wife, Kate. Of the four residences the couple has owned, none has been spared Culpepper's obsession with power tools. He and Kate have two sons: William and David: the first a resident of New Haven, CT, the other a resident of Paris, France.